Y TU MAMÁ TAMBIÉN

Queer Film Classics

Edited by Matthew Hays and Thomas Waugh

The enduring commercial success of LGBTQ2I films over recent generations offers proof of widespread interest in queer film within both pop culture and academia. Not only are recent works riding the wave of the new maturity of queer film culture, but a century of queer and proto-queer classics are in busy circulation thanks to a burgeoning online queer cinephile culture and have been brought back to life by omnipresent festivals and revivals. Meditations on individual films from queer perspectives are particularly urgent, unlocking new understandings of political as well as aesthetic and personal concerns.

Queer Film Classics at McGill-Queen's University Press emphasizes good writing, rigorous but accessible scholarship, and personal, reflective thinking about the significance of each film – writing that is true to the film, original, and enlightening and enjoyable for film buffs, scholars, and students alike. Books in the series are short – roughly 40,000 words – but well illustrated and allow for considerable depth. Exploring historical, authorial, and production contexts and drawing on filmic analysis, these open-ended essays also develop the author's personal interests or a subjective reading of the work's sexual identity discourses or reception. The series aims to meet the diversity, quality, and originality of classics in the queer film canon, broadly conceived, with equally compelling writing and critical insight. Books in the series have much to teach us, not only about the art of film but about the queer ways in which films can transmit our meanings, our stories, and our dreams.

Y TU MAMÁ TAMBIÉN

Juan Llamas-Rodriguez

McGill-Queen's University Press

Montreal & Kingston | London | Chicago

ISBN 978-0-2280-2378-4 (cloth)
ISBN 978-0-2280-2379-1 (paper)
ISBN 978-0-2280-2403-3 (ePDF)
ISBN 978-0-2280-2404-0 (ePUB)

Legal deposit first quarter 2025
Bibliothèque nationale du Québec

Printed in Canada on acid-free paper that is 100% ancient forest free
(100% post-consumer recycled), processed chlorine free

McGill-Queen's University Press in Montreal is on land which long
served as a site of meeting and exchange amongst Indigenous Peoples,
including the Haudenosaunee and Anishinabeg nations. In Kingston it is
situated on the territory of the Haudenosaunee and Anishinaabek. We
acknowledge and thank the diverse Indigenous Peoples whose footsteps
have marked these territories on which peoples of the world now gather.

Library and Archives Canada Cataloguing in Publication

Title: Y tu mamá también / Juan Llamas-Rodriguez.
Names: Llamas-Rodriguez, Juan, author.
Series: Queer film classics (McGill-Queen's University Press)
Description: Series statement: Queer film classics | Includes bibliograph-
  ical references and index.
Identifiers: Canadiana (print) 20240473450 | Canadiana (ebook)
  20240473469 | ISBN 9780228023784 (cloth) | ISBN 9780228023791
  (paper) | ISBN 9780228024033 (ePDF) | ISBN 9780228024040 (ePUB)
Subjects: LCSH: Y tu mamá también (Motion picture) | LCSH: Coming-
  of-age films—History and criticism.
Classification: LCC PN1997.Y24 L53 2025 | DDC 791.43/72—dc23

This book was designed and typeset by studio oneonone in Minion 11/14.
Copyediting by Kathryn Simpson.

Contents

Acknowledgments

Despite the single author credit on its cover, this book would not have been possible without the support and encouragement of multiple people. Consider these a few "wandering camera" moments to spotlight those who accompanied me on the formative road trip that was the creation of this book.

First I must acknowledge the many friends who have watched *Y Tu Mamá También* with me and shared their (positive and negative) thoughts throughout the years, particularly Andrea Cerón, Philippe Signoret, Elisa Iannacone, Wesley Jacks. I could not have asked for a better friend and colleague to develop my intellectual fascination with this film than Brandon Arroyo, who first invited me to lecture on it for his "Sexual Representation in Cinema" course and who has continued to commiserate with me about the many achievements of the film. I am also thankful to Brandon for suggesting I submit a proposal to write about the film for the QFC series.

The editors of the Queer Film Classics series, Thomas Waugh and Matthew Hays, have been unreserved champions of this project from the beginning. I am incredibly grateful for their unwavering support and careful feedback throughout. It has also been a joy to work with editor Jonathan Crago and the team at McGill-Queen's University Press.

The research for this book would not have been possible without the support of the staff at the Cineteca Nacional in Mexico City, the archives of the

Toronto International Film Festival, and the University of Pennsylvania libraries. An early version of the argument developed in chapter 2 was first presented at a virtual colloquium of the British Audio-Visual Research Network in fall 2021. Thank you to the colloquium organizers and to those in attendance for their thoughtful suggestions.

This book was revised and finished during my year-long fellowship at the Institute for Advanced Study in Princeton. I am thankful to the staff and faculty of the IAS for creating a space conducive to writing and thinking. And I am eternally grateful to the cohort of Latin American fellows there – particularly Antonio Vázquez-Arroyo and Jennifer Duprey – for their camaraderie and encouragement during the last few weeks finalizing the manuscript.

Finally, thanks to my partner Gabe for his continued support in small and big ways – and for putting up with me going on and on about *Y Tu Mamá También* for over three years. What a ride it has been.

Synopsis

In Mexico City, teenage friends Tenoch Iturbide and Julio Zapata idly spend their summer months before college while their respective girlfriends are travelling together through Europe. At a lavish family wedding, the boys meet Luisa Cortés, the beautiful twenty-something wife of Tenoch's cousin Jano, who has just moved to Mexico from Spain. Tenoch and Julio try to impress Luisa by inviting her on a trip to the most beautiful, secluded beach in Mexico called *la Boca del Cielo* (Heaven's Mouth), a beach that, in reality, does not exist. After learning of Jano's latest marital indiscretion, Luisa takes Tenoch and Julio's offer to go along on this road trip.

The boys quickly pull together a road trip to a non-existent beach and the three protagonists set off driving through rural Mexico. They pass the time by talking about their relationships and sexual experiences. While the boys boast about their exploits, overselling their modest set of sexual encounters, Luisa speaks more measuredly about Jano and her first teenage love, who died in an accident.

On an overnight stop, Luisa telephones Jano to leave a goodbye note on his answering machine. Tenoch goes to her motel room looking for shampoo and finds her crying. She comes onto him, and he awkwardly but enthusiastically has sex with her. Julio sees this from the open doorway and angrily tells Tenoch that he's had sex with his girlfriend. Luisa notices the change in the boys' attitude at dinner, and the next day she tries to even the score by having sex with

Julio. Upset by this, Tenoch then reveals he had sex with Julio's girlfriend. The boys begin to fight verbally, and come close to a physical fight, but Luisa threatens to leave them and institutes new rules for the rest of their trip.

By chance they find an isolated beach coincidentally called Boca del Cielo. The trio gradually relaxes, enjoying the beach and the company of a local family. Luisa makes a final phone call to Jano. That evening, the three drink excessively and joke recklessly about their sexual transgressions, revealing that the two boys have frequently had sex with the same women. "Y tu mamá también," Julio tells Tenoch, indicating he has also slept with Tenoch's mother. The three dance together sensually, then retire to their room. They begin to undress and grope drunkenly, the boys first focusing their attention on Luisa. As she kneels off camera to stimulate them both, they gasp, lean into each other, and kiss passionately.

The next morning, the boys wake up together, naked. They immediately turn away from each other and express eagerness to return home. Luisa stays behind to explore the beaches. Upon their return to Mexico City, the boys break up with their girlfriends and stop hanging out with each other.

The final scene follows Tenoch and Julio's chance encounter a year later, in 2000, the year that the Institutional Revolutionary Party lost the first presidential election in seventy-one years. They have a cup of coffee together and catch up on each other's lives. Tenoch informs Julio that Luisa died of cancer a month after their trip, and that she knew she was ill during the trip. Tenoch excuses himself; Julio asks for the cheque; the narrator informs us that they will never see each other again.

Credits

Y Tu Mamá También, 2001, Mexico, Spanish, 106 minutes [100 minutes US cut version], colour, sound, Arriflex 35 IIC, 1.85:1
Filmed in Mexico: Mexico City, Tepelmeme Villa de Morelos, Huatulco, and Puerto Escondido
MPAA Rating: R
Production Company: Anhelo Producciones

Director: Alfonso Cuarón
Screenwriters: Alfonso Cuarón, Carlos Cuarón
Producers: Alfonso Cuarón, Jorge Vergara
Executive Producers: Sergio Aguero, Amy Kaufman, David Linde
Director of Photography: Emmanuel Lubezki
Production Designers: Marc Bedia, Miguel Ángel Álvarez
Editors: Alfonso Cuarón, Alex Rodríguez
Casting Director: Manuel Teil
Costume Designer: Gabriela Diaque
Sound: José Antonio García
Art Directors: Guillermo Cossío, Diana Quiroz, Miguel Ángel Álvarez
Set Decorator: Roberto Loera

Principal Cast

Maribel Verdú	Luisa Cortés
Gael García Bernal	Julio Zapata
Diego Luna	Tenoch Iturbide
Daniel Giménez Cacho	Narrator
Ana López Mercado	Ana Morelos
Arturo Ríos	Esteban Morelos
María Aura	Cecilia Huerta
Nathan Grinberg	Manuel Huerta
Verónica Langer	María Eugenia Calles de Huerta
Giselle Audirac	Nicole Bazaine
Andrés Almeida	Diego "Saba" Madero
Diana Bracho	Silvia Allende de Iturbide
Emilio Echevarría	Miguel Iturbide
Marta Aura	Enriqueta "Queta" Allenda
Juan Carlos Remolina	Alejandro "Jano" Montes de Oca
Liboria Rodríguez	Leodegaria "Leo" Victoria
Silverio Palacios	Jesús "Chuy" Carranza
Mayra Sérbulo	Mabel Juárez de Carranza
Andrea López	Lucero Carranza
Amaury Sérbulo	Christian Carranza
Jorge Vergara	President

World Premiere: 8 June 2001
Distributors: Twentieth Century Fox (North America)
DVD release: MGM Home Entertainment (2002), The Criterion Collection (2014)

Y TU MAMÁ TAMBIÉN

Introduction
Queering a *Charolastra* Film Classic

The first time I watched *Y Tu Mamá También* (2001), it was on a bootleg VHS
tape I borrowed from a high school friend. One night in fall 2002, after the
rest of my family had gone to sleep, I sat in front of the 13″ television I had in
my room, plugged my headphones into the player's auxiliary port, and
popped the tape into the dual VCR-DVD player. My friend had recorded the
film when it aired on cable a few weeks earlier. Because they had no other
blank VHS at the time – or, perhaps, as a stealth strategy to hide the bootleg
recording – the film began halfway through a recording of the mass that Pope
John Paul II officiated that summer in Mexico City for the canonization of
St Juan Diego. As the pope raises the consecrated host at the altar, the video
cuts to a quick second of static and then to the roaming camera making its
way into the bedroom where Diego Luna, as Tenoch, is finishing having sex
with his girlfriend.

I have often thought about this fortuitous introduction to the film as I have
rewatched and written about it throughout the years. The method through
which I acquired a copy of *Y Tu Mamá También* was not entirely unlike how
other teenagers at the time also watched it. The controversial "C" rating of
the film (for adults over eighteen years only) both raised the popular profile
of the film and prevented young audiences from accessing it at the movie theatre. Mexican critics at the time already subtly suggested that teenagers would
"find an ingenious way to watch it" (Arredondo 2001) or unsubtly bemoaned

that "a pirate copy surely already circulates" (Celin 2001). Although my bor-rowed pirated copy of the film would not come until over a year after its orig-inal release, the illicit thrill of that initial viewing mimicked the same sense of transgression and youthful recklessness the film captured in the summer of 2001.

Responses from audiences, critics, international festivals, and academic writers alike have long circled around the film's undoing, transgressing, and/or merging of Mexican national identity traditions with a "new" global millennial sexuality. That bootleg copy's unintentional smash cut from a close-up of Pope John Paul II raising the consecrated host to the voyeuristic pan and push into Diego Luna's bare ass seared in my mind the daring spirit captured by the film that would lead it to become an international sensation. Little did I know at the time the privileged place it would later come to occupy in the world travels of its stars, its filmmakers, and Mexican media at large.

Nowadays I own six copies of *Y Tu Mamá También*: three DVDs (for regions 1, 2, and 4); the Blu-ray special Criterion Collection edition; and two digital copies (720p and 4K). None of these hold the same emotional weight as that first bootleg VHS, which I suspect has long been discarded. While these digital copies hold little of the "inherent properties of degeneration" of the analogue VHS (Hilderbrand 2009, 6), I also appreciate how the advent of digital tech-nologies for reproducing copies of the film and the access to networked plat-forms to circulate these copies has impacted the enduring popularity and legacy of the film. Attending to this new media landscape, this book revisits a classic of New Mexican Cinema from the vantage point granted by two-plus decades of social, industrial, and technological changes. My goal is to advocate for this film's status as a queer film classic by demonstrating how a critical analysis of its textual features, reception history, and sociocultural impact continue to offer valuable insights to both queer studies and media studies. It is now a quite different twenty-first-century world than the one *Y Tu Mamá También* first burst into, yet its queer legacies have only continued to grow.

A Popular Hit

Y Tu Mamá También tells the story of Tenoch and Julio, two teenage lifelong friends from different classes in Mexico City who spend their summer days masturbating, smoking pot, and relaxing at Tenoch's family country club while their girlfriends are away in Europe. At a family wedding, they meet the Spaniard Luisa and invite her to come with them on a road trip to Boca del Cielo, a secluded beach they have made up. Surprisingly, she accepts, so the trio borrow a station wagon from Julio's sister and drive across the country. Throughout the trip, they swap stories about their sexual pasts. Luisa has sex with Tenoch and then with Julio, provoking a long-simmering rivalry that leads them to confess the many transgressions to their infamous friend code (the *charolastra* manifesto), including the fact that both have slept with each other's girlfriends. After a period of animosity, the trio makes up when they finally discover the (actually real) Boca del Cielo and, one drunken celebratory night, have sex together. Visibly shaken the morning after, Tenoch and Julio head back to Mexico City while Luisa stays in the beach town. A year later, the now estranged friends randomly meet up and catch up. Julio learns that Luisa had late-stage cancer all along and decided to stay in Boca del Cielo until she died. The film's narrator tells us that Tenoch and Julio will never see each other again.

A fairly straightforward plot description such as this one does not do justice to the multiple themes and artistic achievements the film weaves together. While remaining a teen sex comedy at heart, the film is also an accomplished indictment of Mexican society at the turn of the twenty-first century. Its direction, cinematography, acting, and writing were widely recognized at the time and have been analyzed extensively in the decades since its release. Undoubtedly, it was a mixture of generic appeal, creative filmmaking, and formidable timing that turned what could have been another simple road trip movie into a national and then international hit.

The film was a sensation from the moment it premiered in Mexico in summer 2001. Its promotional campaign included "ads and billboards absolutely everywhere, from bus stops, metro stations and public transportation to every imaginable free space" in overcrowded Mexico City (Shaw 2013, 180). The controversy over the "C" rating, including the filmmakers' vocal rebukes of the rating decision, fuelled the expectations for the film. In its opening weekend, it became the top-grossing opening for a Mexican film. It later broke Mexico's box office record for a domestic film, which had been set by the equally popular *Amores Perros* (2000) the year before.

In the United States, *Y Tu Mamá También* debuted at an event organized by New York City's Guggenheim Museum, the Mexican Cultural Institute, and Cinema Tropical. Originally meant to be distributed to arthouse theatres and markets with predominantly Mexican audiences, the film was soon requested by major theatre chains and quickly broke into the mainstream. Executives from IFC, which distributed *Y Tu Mamá También* in the United States, praised its crossover appeal, stating that the film "broke away from the foreign-language market and showed that a Spanish-language film is not a foreign-language [movie] in the US" (Miller et al. 2011). It played in over forty countries and grossed over US$33.5 million worldwide.

According to scholar Sergio de la Mora, there was so much buzz about *Y Tu Mamá También* during its premiere screening at the 2001 International Festival of New Latin American Cinema in Havana that a riot almost broke out among those waiting in line outside the Yara theatre: "I witnessed more than fifteen hundred people standing in line for over two hours waiting to get into the screening. As the crowd grew beyond normal proportions and more film fans pressed against the glass doors at the lobby of the Yara, the pressure caused the glass to shatter. When the police arrived, the screening was canceled and the huge crowd was dispersed into the rain-slicked streets of La Habana on that memorable overcast evening in December (2009, 169)." Among the film's international recognitions were awards for Best Screenplay and Best Newcomers (for Diego Luna and Gael García Bernal) at the Venice International Film Festival; the FIPRESCI Prize at the Havana Film Festival; Best Original Screenplay nominations from both the BAFTAS and the Oscars; Best Foreign Language Film nominations from the Golden Globes and Independent Spirit Awards; and recognitions from several critics' societies in the United States.

For Mexican writer Carlos Monsiváis (2001), the popularity of *Y Tu Mamá También* and *Amores Perros* lay in their creative mobilization of local particularities to achieve global resonance. In a "180-degree turn" from an earlier Mexican cinema that "directed itself to an international audience from the start," these new films were "shamelessly conceived from within a specific public and addressed to audiences everywhere that share their notions of speed, frank sexuality, and speech patterns undisturbed by formal concerns." The success of this new Mexican cinema was its frankness as a "bellicose adaptation of the local" to the "behavioral laws of globalization" (Monsiváis 2001).

The film was an important milestone for many of those involved – at least the men. It earned Alfonso Cuarón his first Academy Award nomination, now one of many. Following the premiere of Cuarón's widely acclaimed film *Roma* in 2018, auteurist fans and critics alike turned back to *Y Tu Mamá También* to trace how the filmmaker's aesthetic and social concerns had long been present in the earlier film. As explored in depth in chapter 2, the use of a popular song by Mexican singer Marco Antonio Solís in the film also represented a turning point for the artist's move to transnational appeal. And of course, the film launched the international careers of Mexican actors Gael García Bernal and Diego Luna, both of whom went on to work extensively not only in Hollywood but also with major international filmmakers across Argentina, Spain, France, and Cuba.

A Queer Legacy

"It's hard to explain; it's a Mexican idiosyncrasy, but you're more macho if you fuck men, you know?" Gael García Bernal marvels in the "Rants and Raves" section of the May 2002 issue of *The Advocate*. This idiosyncrasy becomes less hard to explain when we account for how the concept of manhood in Mexican culture remains entangled with Octavio Paz's legacy in his classic oeuvre *El Laberinto de la Soledad* (1950). In the chapter "Hijos de la Malinche," Paz posits that Mexican men engage in a constant defensive struggle to keep themselves closed, to avoid vulnerability, by instead focusing on *chingar* (to fuck, to fuck over). Men assert their masculinity by proving themselves to be *grandes chingones* over other men and over women. Between men, one can attain an image of superiority by symbolically cracking his cohort; he can chingar his rival and make himself *el gran chingón*, and his rival *el chingado*. His rival is symbolically penetrated and feminized in this losing encounter. For Paz, this masculine display of force is always sexualized. Competitive masculine relations in Mexico, then, take on homosexual overtones. The macho's need to prove his masculinity by asserting his superiority over other men invariably implies a homosexual relation of chingar in which the penetrated man, the loser in the competitive encounter, actually becomes symbolically homosexual.

Whether by theorizing the implicit misogyny in this dynamic (Monsiváis 2013), addressing its complex implications of sexual violence (Irwin 2003), or recuperating the role of the *pasivo* (bottom) from within it (Cervantez-Gomez 2020), Mexican cultural theorists must contend with the legacy of Paz's originary paradox: Mexican masculinity as always already homosocial and hypersexualized. Not surprisingly, the conceptual framework laid out by Octavio Paz and reworked by various other scholars across the decades has long proven generative for the analysis of the sexual and gender politics of *Y Tu Mamá También* (Acevedo-Muñoz 2004; Bertrán 2009; Hind 2004a; Torres

San Martín 2016; Worrell 2011). The film's lambasting of its male protagonists' sexual inadequacies signalled a potential cinematic reckoning with Mexican masculinities at the turn of the new century.

By today's standards, *Y Tu Mamá También* does not espouse a track record that would easily grant it a place in the LGBT+ cinema pantheon. The famous charolastra manifesto[1] created by the film's protagonists includes the maxim "Puto el que le vaya al América" as the sixth and ninth tenets (because it bears repeating), mobilizing the homophobic epithet "puto" here as an insult for the fans of a polarizing soccer team. By nonchalantly reinforcing a long-standing nexus of undesired masculinity and homosexuality in Mexican culture, this formulation also prefigures the arduous struggle throughout the 2010s – by the notoriously unethical FIFA, no less – to convince Mexican fans to stop chanting the epithet at international soccer matches. (Not to mention the controversy over the song "Puto" from Mexican alternative rock band Molotov, co-creators of the original song "Here Comes the Mayo" for the *Y Tu Mamá También* soundtrack.) The film's one supposedly gay character, Daniel, is a spectre who is never seen and only mentioned twice: first listed as part of the charolastra crew despite being a "*desafanado*" (naughty one) inching slowly out of the closet, then referenced at the end of the film as "a total queen" who has been disowned by his dad but remains "very happy" with his new boyfriend. All of these moments may not add up to a very proud gay legacy for the film.

Looking back over twenty years later, it is also notable, though perhaps not surprising, that the film did not rouse more interest in exploring cinematic

1 The origin for this neologism offered by Tenoch and Julio in the film is only partly true: while the characters claim it is a mispronunciation of a lyric that goes "charolastra, charolooo," the Cuarón brothers claim that it came from the nickname for one of their niece's friends who would mispronounce the chorus for Smash Mouth's 1999 hit "All Star" from "hey, now, you're all star" to "hey, now, charalastra" – the changing of the second "a" to "o" was a typo the filmmakers never corrected (see Cuarón and Cuarón 2001, 197).

bisexuality at the time. The initial critical reception and subsequent scholarly analyses (explored in depth in chapter 1) vacillated between reading the three-some at the end of the film as diegetic evidence for the boys' closeted same-sex desire and as a metaphor for masculine repression. The fact that there is scant material in the film to support the reading of Tenoch and Julio as bi-sexual could be attributed either to the filmmaker's intended ambivalence to explore the male characters' complicated feelings for each other or to the characters' own inability to think or act beyond a strict sex/gender binary. This "compulsory monosexuality," as Maria San Filippo (2013) terms it, has only solidified within the film's legacy decades later. Fan texts and other new media remixes (detailed in the conclusion) pick up where the film ends and focus almost exclusively on the two boys and their purportedly tragic love story, essentially ignoring most of their hetero sexcapades detailed in the film. At the same time, the resurgent iconicity of the film's threesome has now be-come a touchstone for other bisexually coded love triangles.

Rather than being legibly classified as gay or bisexual, the film retains a distinct queer legacy because of its initial significance in flouting sexual mores and national stereotypes, and because of how it continues to engender new forms of longing and desire. As I will detail over the next three chapters and the conclusion, the film's sexual content left an indelible initial impact on critics and audiences; its postmodern mixing of genres and film styles further ensconced it as a classic through scholarly analyses; its multimedia lives keep it relevant for audiences too young to experience when it first came out. More than two decades after its original release, the film continues to be featured as a touchstone for queer and sex cinema. For instance, just in 2023, it was

Figures 1–4 *Opposite and following page*
The music video for "Beautiful Soul" (2004) borrows its road trip iconography from *Y Tu Mamá También*, including the station wagon, performing the prank of leaving a friend at the gas station, and taking an impromptu swim in a motel's dirty pool.

included in *IndieWire*'s list of sexiest queer films of all time and in *Esquire UK*'s countdown of the best sex movies ever made (Chapman, Dry, and Lattanzio 2023; Maher and Hess 2023).

The film's impact on teen cultures and sexual discourse was both immediate and enduring. In the few years after its release, several music videos freely borrowed the film's road trip imagery as a grammar for the young people's sexcapades. Australian pop star Natalie Imbruglia, who contributed the song "Cold Air" to *Y Tu Mamá También*'s soundtrack (analyzed in chapter 2), later released the music video for her song "Glorious" (2007) as an homage to the film. More explicitly, the music video for US teen pop sensation Jesse McCartney's *Billboard* Hot 100 hit "Beautiful Soul" (2004) restages multiple key scenes from the film, including the car prank at the gas station, the old woman gifting a doll to the love interest, the leads swimming in a dirty leaves-ridden pool, and the final celebration scenes on the beach.

In January 2024, Gael García Bernal participated in a "Closet Picks" video, a YouTube series hosted by the Criterion Collection that asks filmmakers to choose a few of their favourite films from amongst a closetful containing all the titles in the boutique distribution label. Unsurprisingly, among the films he selects are those he starred in, *Amores Perros* and *Y Tu Mamá También*. For the latter, he recalls that when it first came out, people dismissed it as a teen comedy, but that time has revealed that it is "obviously a very deep film." He also admits that it was here that he "discovered cinema properly," including how to make movies since Cuarón involved his actors in the making of the film. García Bernal ends by claiming that there are two things *Y Tu Mamá También* has that "nowadays very few films have": first, he says, is the freedom that the film exudes, and then he says: "The other thing that is very important is: I want you to tell me which film has made you horny in the last years. There's not many. Actually, there is none. And I miss that from cinema! Because I used to get … I used to learn about stuff when I was a kid watching films. And now, it's like, you don't walk out of the cinema feeling like [inhales deeply] something. And this one does. When you come out of the cinema

Figure 5
During his visit to the Criterion Closet in January 2024, Gael García Bernal selects
Y Tu Mamá También as one of his favourites and explains what it means to him
and to audiences.

watching this, you just want to *live* ... and have sex ... and enjoy and love
people." García Bernal's diagnosis that no film in the twenty-plus years since
Y Tu Mamá También has made him horny was not an uncommon idea by
2024. Critics noted the emergence of a monoculture that fetishized toned
bodies yet downplayed – or outright disavowed – sexual desire (Gomes 2023).
As writer Raquel S. Benedict (2021) put it, the social media obsession with
fitness and beauty regimes, along with movie studios' risk-averse propensity
for franchises and remakes, meant that, in twenty-first-century mainstream
cinema, "everyone is beautiful and no one is horny." By the time the film's
twentieth anniversary rolled around, audiences would find that its sexual freedom and unabashed horniness offered welcome respite from the relative
chastity characteristic of wide releases and streaming originals.

The film also became a millennial touchstone for referencing the two-men,
one-woman sexual and/or romantic triangle. While *Y Tu Mamá También* pre-
dates the advent of social media meme cycles, it experienced a mini-resurgence

with the release of *Challengers* (2024) – Luca Guadagnino's very horny movie about a tennis-world love triangle between Zendaya, Mike Faist, and Josh O'Connor – only a few months after García Bernal's declarations about the paucity of horniness in twenty-first-century cinema. Early social media reactions to the teaser trailer often included a play on words with the title of *Y Tu Mamá También*: Canadian writer Peter Knegt quipped, "It's serving 'Y tu tennis también,'" while US writer Saeed Jones joked, "My Spanish is rusty but … 'Y Tu Zendaya Tambien.'" On opening weekend, film-related Twitter accounts, including that of the Sundance Film Festival, posted screenshots of Luisa, Tenoch, and Julio, labelling them as early precursors to (and perhaps fans of) the *Challengers* threesome.

Another example of the film's enduring legacy lies in the instantly classic sketch "Wells for Boys," which aired on the 3 December 2016 episode of *Saturday Night Live*, the long-running US television comedy series. Written by gay writers Julio Torres and Jeremy Beiler, this parody of a Fisher-Price advertisement focuses on Spencer, a young boy who does not like to play with other kids and instead spends his time with an aquamarine and light gray plastic toy well by leaning on it, contemplating his reflection within it, and whispering secrets into it. While other boys "live unexamined lives," this "sensitive boy" has a "heart full of questions," demurs the commercial's voiceover narrator as the camera moves away from a group of boys shooting each other with water guns towards Spencer sitting next to his well at the far distance. Spencer never speaks; when the narrator prompts us to "hear how much he loves the well," we cut to a shot of Spencer leaning into his mother (played by Emma Stone) and whispering into her sweater. She translates for us that he does not want to do the commercial anymore; then she asks him, "Do you want to watch *Y Tu Mamá También*?"

What makes this punchline work is the jarring disconnect that a foreign film with copious amounts of nudity and sex scenes would be the comfort movie for this quiet, introspective "sensitive boy." Yet the allusion to the film is not for the fictional Spencer himself but for the queer viewers who might empathize with both the desire for a toy that fosters creative introspection and the admiration of a foreign film with copious amounts of nudity and sex scenes. In his review for *The Advocate*, writer Daniel Reynolds (2016) praised the sketch for "nail[ing] the loneliness of queer kids" and listed foremost among its "dog whistles to queer viewers" the fact that Spencer's mother asks "if he might want to watch the queer classic *Y Tu Mamá También*." Fifteen years after its release, the film had settled into its legacy as a queer classic and a touchstone for sensitive boys' coming-of-age, one that could easily show up in popular TV shows as a queer wink to the knowing audience.

This handful of examples illustrates how the film's queer legacy extends and endures globally. In fact, I posit that the case for *Y Tu Mamá También* as a "queer film classic" relies more on this global appeal than on its standing within a specific lineage of queer Mexican cinema. A distinct history of Mexican queer cinema would most likely focus on classics such as *El Lugar Sin Límites* (Arturo Ripstein, 1978) and *Doña Herlinda y su Hijo* (Jaime Humberto Hermosillo, 1985) and on the extended oeuvres of Julián Hernández's art-house films, Manolo Cano's camp flicks, and Mecos Film's porn romps.[2] While remaining a distinctly Mexican production, the international reach of *Y Tu Mamá También* throughout the years – including its stars, filmmakers, paratexts, and new media remixes – positions the film as a global queer film classic.

Not surprisingly, the film has attracted plenty of critical and academic analyses, as I detail in chapter 1. These many responses and appraisals certainly speak to the film's multi-layered artistry and socio-cultural relevance, yet such a plethora of writing reaches a point where, to borrow a quote from the film, we are all just swirling around someone else's atole. Given this already rich scholarly trove, my intentions in writing this book have less to do

2 In the conclusion to his analysis of Mexican queer media production in the twenty-first century, Paul Julian Smith (2017) also offers other texts that could be reincorporated into an expanded history of Mexican national queer cinema.

with arguing for a cinematic canon where *Y Tu Mamá También* would fit in and even less with tracing how it prefigures the development of Alfonso Cuarón's auteurist bona fides. There have been at least two other monographs dedicated exclusively to the film and, in their own ways, both painstakingly detail the film's many formal achievements and marvel at Cuarón's directorial style (Baugh 2019; Smith 2022). While the antecedents and later developments in Cuarón's filmography certainly inform my analysis of *Y Tu Mamá También*, I avoid the hagiographical approach of these other monographs on the film.

Instead, my goal here is to invite readers to look back at the film as both a significant product of its time and a shifting cultural object that continues to resonate with audiences. In retrospect, the film astutely captures a moment in Mexican history, politically and cinematically. It also represents a turning point for Mexican stardom on the world stage and instigates a reframing of millennial Mexican masculinities more broadly. While new historical and textual analyses of queerness in Mexican and Latin American cinema tend to emphasize issues of identity and representation, my approach to *Y Tu Mamá También* as a "queer classic," in contrast, emphasizes queer affects, queer forms of reading, and queering as remix across the analyses of the film's text, reception, and circulation. A point I emphasize throughout is that the film's queer legacy cannot be fully understood without seriously considering its reverberations through other media, especially music and social media platforms. Over two decades after its release, the film continues to teach us how to find queer resonances across national and international film styles and to imagine queer media as complex networks of influence and rediscovery.

A Personal Touchstone

Y Tu Mamá También holds a privileged place for me not only as a queer Mexican man but also as a global media scholar. It was perhaps the last film I systematically thought and wrote about as a film scholar while completing a master's in film studies at Concordia University in 2013 before turning towards television and new media forms for my doctoral studies.

As a new graduate student, I wrote a seminar paper about how the film's mainstream and academic reception tested the limits of what critical scholars in several humanities fields were considering a "transnational turn," a move to think beyond the idea of the nation as a prism through which to analyze culture. The leftovers of those initial ideas – minus a significant portion of the niche academic baggage, hopefully – constitute the discussion of the reception of the film in chapter 1. First, I turn to Mexican critics' reactions to the film when it first premiered. Based on archival research, I demonstrate how the reception from Mexican critics, both proponents and detractors, reveals an intense desire to playfully engage with its sexual themes – an invitation to audiences to also engage in a plethora of queer modes of reception. Second, I offer a brief overview of the film's scholarly reception in the two decades since its release. This overview traces a shift from analyses that focus on revisionist readings of the Mexican nation and its macho-based masculinity to analyses exploring the transnational appeal of the film. Here I suggest that the intellectual reappraisal of the film by critics and scholars also hindered discussions about its sexual frankness, a tendency that has only recently begun to be overturned.

Chapter 2 focuses on what I consider to be a still underexamined feature of the film that sheds light on its significance as a queer film classic. In the nearly hundred texts about the film I have read, including press reviews, academic articles, blog posts, and other assorted writings, the film's soundtrack barely earns a passing mention. I propose to remedy this oversight. A close reading of the film through its soundtrack reveals the creation of a queer sensibility that inflects the film's much-lauded merging of youth sexual liberation with national societal decay. Song choices, along with the narrator's commentary, likewise draw attention to the ways that *time drags*, that is, how the legacy of the past continues to shape the present and how the sense of the future dotes the present with an anticipatory charge. These temporal overlaps also present a queer mode of reception by perverting the neat distinctions between the past, present, and future. To further emphasize the drag of time, I propose that the film's sonic appeal becomes all the more pronounced and powerful with repeated viewings.

My first-ever academic guest lecture was when I was a teaching assistant for the course "Sexual Representation in Film" at Concordia University. In that lecture, I sought to demonstrate to students how *Y Tu Mamá También* instantiated a new way to watch and desire Mexican masculinities, one that connected to classical cinema tropes but refashioned them for the twenty-first century. These ideas shape chapter 3. Often credited as the launching pad for Gael García Bernal's and Diego Luna's international careers, the film also represents a turning point for the international imagination of Mexican male actors. The international press coverage of the film's stars reveals an early struggle to address their sexual appeal, resorting to dated and racist tropes that quickly proved insufficient to capture the allure of these millennial masculinities. Yet the film's unabashed playfulness with and celebration of its protagonists' bodies teaches us how to embrace their newfound sexual appeal, one that breaks with the traditional ideals of Mexican men – and rebrands them as an ethnically ambiguous object for international desire.

The book ends where most people's memories of the film begin. In the conclusion, I focus exclusively on the most famous scene in the film, the kiss between Tenoch and Julio during the climactic threesome. I first explore the moment's initial controversial reception, then its resurgent popularity decades later, and, finally, its remixing on social media platforms. The short history of this famous kiss offers a final summary of the themes explored throughout the book: the back-and-forth swings in the film's reception, the affective resonance of its melodramatic musical cues, and the international relevance of its portrayals of masculinity.

Ten years after finishing my master's program, writing this book has been a welcome opportunity to revisit a cultural text that had both sensual appeal in my teenage years and intellectual appeal in my early adulthood through the eyes of a more seasoned (some might say cynical) media scholar. "Pop mata poesía," reads the third tenet of the charolastra manifesto. I hope to illustrate both the pop and the poetry of *Y Tu Mamá También* in the pages that follow.

Chapter 1
"Un Chorreo de Semen en la Alberca": Sexual Language Games in Film Reception

The seventh point in the charolastra manifesto declares, "¡Qué muera la moral! y ¡Qué viva la chaqueta!" The film's English subtitles translate this phrase as "Whacking off rules," a poor facsimile that misses the rhetorical flourish and gleeful sentiment of the original declaration. The colloquial expression "que viva" better approximates the enthusiasm of saying "Long live __!" At the same time, its pairing with the antonymic "que muera" emphasizes that for masturbation to live, morality must die. "Whacking off rules" simply fails to account for the celebration and the caution of the original declaration. This minor instance of mistranslation reveals a basic fact: how we *talk* about sex shapes the social, affective, or ideological impact of sex. How we talk about sex in *Y Tu Mamá También* remains a crucial aspect in revisiting the critical reception of the film two decades later. Language games prove to be a structuring frame for the reception of the film's sexual scenes and thematics, not only in terms of a mismatch between different linguistic usages but also in the back-and-forth between the film's language – what sex the film presents, and how – and the critical takes about that sex.

"¡Qué muera la moral! y ¡Qué viva la chaqueta!" offers a rejoinder for how audiences should approach the film: to embrace its (literal and figurative) masturbatory elements in order to appreciate its broader cultural work. For many scholars, there has always been an implicit insistence on explaining how the characters' conversations about and depictions of sex speak to the broader metaphorical, conceptual, or ideological concerns of the film. Yet, as Scott Baugh argues, international reviews of the film unduly emphasized the issue of sex by claiming the film was "wildly erotic" and its sex scenes "steamy" (2020, 60). Through his own close textual analysis of the sex in the film, Baugh frames such assessments as out of proportion, arguing instead that the clumsiness and awkwardness of the sex scenes – not to mention their anticlimactically quick denouements – often evidence a more realist than sensualist approach. The enthusiastic overselling of its sex scenes could be explained as a by-product of its promotional campaign or the aforementioned controversy over the "C" rating in Mexico. Even if the initial critical reception did pump up the eroticism and steaminess of the sex in *Y Tu Mamá También* beyond what the film itself presented to audiences, its legacy owes much to how critics and scholars have made (literal and figurative) sense of those sex scenes.

In this chapter, I focus on three moments of the film's reception to draw attention to the multiple different ways that audiences, critics, and scholars have engaged with the film's sex. First, the mainstream and critical reception in Mexico upon its release in summer 2001; second, the international reception in film festivals that summer and in spring 2002; and third, the (mostly Anglophone) scholarly analysis of the film throughout the 2000s and 2010s. Across these different moments, the film's sex meant different things for the different groups. For some, the film's directness was crass and distasteful. For others, their recollections helped conjure up an alternative "wildly erotic" version of the film. For still others, especially many of the academic critics in the decades since the film's release, the sex is metaphorical. Previous article- and book-length accounts of *Y Tu Mamá También* have already covered these differences in the film's national and transnational reception, yet most of these authors merely describe the film's reception as a matter of historical context. My goal in this chapter, instead, is to pursue *a queer reading of said reception*, theorizing critics' reviews, festival copy, and scholarly writings as para-texts that, in form and content, influence how we make sense of the film's sexual materials. To understand the legacy of *Y Tu Mamá También* as a queer film classic, we must appreciate its initial and enduring impact in getting critics and audiences to play with, think through, and see beyond its sex comedy antics.

Sex for Teens, Too Much Sex, Not the Right Sex! (Local Reception)

There is no better way to begin an overview of the reception from Mexican critics than with arts editor Jorge Dorantes's enthusiastic early review "Por qué es grande *Y tu mamá también*" (Why *Y Tu Mamá También* is great), published in the periodical *El Economista* two weeks before the release of the film. According to his review, Dorantes had access to an early cut of the film because a friend of his was working on the design of the film's poster and he waited until the day of the film's press junket to release his glowing assessment. He specifically draws attention to the sex scenes as one of the things that make *Y Tu Mamá También* great, calling them "the best sex scenes in our [Mexican] cinema" with the caveat that "while this fact can be disputed, [this statement] demonstrates my enthusiasm for *Y Tu Mamá También*'s 'bedding' scenes (though not all of them take place on a bed)." After lauding Maribel Verdú's performance in the sex scenes, Dorantes concludes that there is "a certain nakedness (in a metaphorical sense), a mix of innocence and perversion, in the sex scenes that seems unprecedented in [Mexican] cinema" (2001a, 59).[1]

---

1 All translations from sources originally in Spanish are my own. I retain some of the original terms when the proposed translation does not fully encapsulate the sense of the term in Mexican Spanish.

While few were as nakedly effusive as Dorantes, other Mexican critics likewise wrote positive reviews of the film. Critics characterized it as "humorous, ironic, and intelligent" (Melche 2001), "unmissable" (Celin 2001), "entertaining and sobering" (Alvarado 2001), "an enjoyable story that captures viewers between laughter and amazement" (Arredondo 2001), "an incisive vision of our current reality" (Naime 2001), "an emotional and funny film that captures the feeling of a generation" (Aviña 2001).

Critics' evaluations of the sex scenes varied widely. In the country's major newspaper *Reforma*, critic Eduardo Alvarado described the film's opening with Tenoch and his girlfriend as "a rude scene of teenage sex, truly animalistic, clumsy and wretched, that will please the hordes of *mochos* [prudes] newly out of the closet" (2001, 21). Alvarado also wonders, but never resolves, whether there had ever been a threesome in a Mexican film before. Despite praising the film overall, X. Andrés Naime characterizes it as "so crude that you cannot believe what you are watching" and concludes that perhaps "that morbid fascination for the sexual and the erotic – including the countless naked bodies – will keep filling movie theaters all summer" (2001, 21). A less enthusiastic (and unattributed) review in the periodical *Milenio* describes the film as "obscene but not spicy, sexually aggressive and not at all erotic, albeit ultimately hyperrealist" and assumes, somewhat condescendingly, that such mundane explicitness would "speak directly to youths around the same age as the protagonists" (2001, 12).

Indeed, several critics ended their reviews by lamenting that the "C" rating (restricted to ages eighteen and up) would keep the film away from its most appropriate audience: teenagers. In the national newspapers, critic Rafael Aviña (2001) of *Reforma* called out the RTC as "prudish" while Fernando Celin (2001) of *Novedades* referred to the classification as "a refined form of censorship."

Bemoaning the restrictive rating proved mostly unnecessary since the controversy surrounding it turned out to be the best free advertisement for the film. While the marketing strategy of framing the film as provocative and edgy sparked initial interest within the general Mexican public, it was the ratings board's repeated warnings that this rating would be strictly enforced at the theatres that ultimately raised the film to its apex of popular success.

Such widespread popularity presented a challenge for theatre managers who sought to convey to patrons, via interviews with the press, that they merely enforced the rules handed down by the ratings board. This apologetic signalling reflected a fear that audiences would take out their frustrations with the rating on the theatre staff. Though perhaps overstated, a few days after the premiere, there were some stories circulating about hordes of high school students overpowering the staff and gaining entry to watch the film in Cinépolis theatres in the downtown area of Mexico City (Huerta 2001).

Audiences certainly expressed their discontent with the rating and its enforcement in theatres. An article published in *Reforma* just days after the release of the film quotes several young people's reactions to the ratings board's insistence that theatre staff must police who was allowed to watch the film. A fifteen-year-old woman advocates that she and her peers "are not lacking in judgment for being underage. We know what will affect us and what will not." After her friend was denied entry because he forgot his photo ID, a nineteen-year-old woman expresses frustration because "one can watch worse things on television and in the streets, but they only restrict it here [in the theatres]." A twenty-year-old man goes further to critique institutional oversight, claiming that the Mexican authorities "should worry about creating jobs and enriching the country, rather than dictating these laws that are no use to anyone" (Huerta 2001). Indeed, for many Mexicans the RTC was a metonym for the conservative values of the new Vicente Fox administration, whose election is signalled at the end of *Y Tu Mamá También*. The *Reforma* article pointedly ends by quoting the sole theatre patron in favour of the restrictive rating: "'There are those that only want to watch sex scenes and will damage themselves by doing so. I think there should be [admission] controls against that,' considered Arturo Olguín, age 43, as he entered the late-night showing of *Y Tu Mamá También* at Cinemex Palacio Chino" (Huerta 2001).

In spite of these popular celebrations, the early critical reception of the film was not always positive and sometimes veered into unnecessarily spiteful. The two most notable of these negative reviews are also among the most cited in academic scholarship of the film: Leonardo García Tsao in *La Jornada* and Jorge Ayala Blanco in *El Financiero*. As Mexican film critic Fernanda Solórzano would argue in her assessment a year later, the viciousness of this negative critical response could be partly explained by a plethora of extratextual factors, most of them inherited from a time when critics were called upon to be the voice of (moral and aesthetic) authority on exclusively national cinematic productions. That is, when faced with a film deemed a *national* production, certain Mexican critics' response to the film text itself would be marked by issues such as whether it was state or privately funded, whether the director is part of a family of respected artists, or whether rival critics have already formed an opinion on the film (Solórzano 2002).

When other scholars point to García Tsao's and Ayala Blanco's reviews as evidence of the mixed reception of the film, they tend to take the negative assessments seriously as aesthetic judgments (Baugh 2021; Smith 2022). I am less interested in straightforwardly engaging with these two reviewers' assessments of the qualities of the film than in queerly reading into the men's inordinate obsession with the sex depicted therein. This obsession was paradoxically evidenced, on the one hand, in their performative distaste for the sex presented in the film yet, on the other hand, in the use of sexual language games in their reviews.

García Tsao titles his review "Solo con tu pajero," a pun on Alfonso Cuarón's first feature, *Solo con Tu Pareja* (1990), that switches the "partner" (*pareja*) of the original title with "masturbator" (*pajero*). The opening sentences make note of the much more positive critical and popular reception of the new film compared to Cuarón's earlier work ten years prior yet insist that *Y Tu Mamá También* only "endorses the usual scourges." Although the characterization of the film as a *versión chilanga* (Mexico City version) of *Beavis and Butthead* has been the most quoted line in the review, it is his al-

Figure 6
While Luisa sits on the bed in the background, still fully clothed, she stares at – and thereby redirects our gaze back to – a fully naked Tenoch in the foreground right.

lusion to porn magazines later in that same sentence that best evidences his reductive take on the film's sex scenes: "a sexist fantasy worthy of the *Penthouse* letters to the editor ('when I got out of the bathroom, the Spaniard showed me her breasts, took off my towel, and started to suck me off')" (García Tsao 2001a, 15).

The explicit description of how this reviewer imagines the sex scene with Tenoch and Luisa would read on the page reveals his identificatory alignment. Rhetorically, the first-person description suggests that García Tsao takes on the position of the young man. The content of that description then incorrectly retells what we *actually* see on screen: a two-shot with Luisa in the background, still fully clothed, staring at – and thereby redirecting our gaze back to – a fully naked Tenoch in the foreground right. Luisa first asks to see Tenoch's penis and instructs him to jerk himself off. It is only after he hesitates and fails to do anything with his penis that she offers to show him her breasts. In his faux *Penthouse* letter to the editor, García Tsao's disdain for the sex scenes colours his recollections of the formal strategies of the film. His account reads more like what a young man might exaggeratedly recount to his buddies after the fact to forget his own inadequacies in the moment.

García Tsao published a shortened, English-language version of his review in the July issue of *Variety* a month later. In this latter version, the allusion to porn only reads, "The mature woman is a sexist fantasy straight out of *Penthouse*," thus depriving readers of the reviewer's slapdash attempts at juvenile sex fanfiction. The English-language version also repeats García Tsao's conclusion from the Spanish-language review that the film's attitude towards sex is moralistic and not liberatory, stating that the film "does not have a laissez-faire attitude about sex" because the end "casts a moralistic, guilt-ridden shroud over the characters' escapades, stifling any sense of liberation." Again, the reviewer here substitutes moralistic criticism for artistic critique by mistaking the characters' perspective on their own sexcapades as representative of the film's perspective on the story.

The second notable negative review of the film comes from Jorge Ayala Blanco, a critic known for generating controversy with his decisive and derisive takes and for using "elaborate and often aggressive language" in his reviews (Martínez Assad 1992). His review of *Y Tu Mamá También*, published in the periodical *El Financiero*, deserves further scrutiny not only for its general dismissal of the film but also for its rhetorical obsession with the film's sexual content despite the critic's purported distaste for it.

In a single, two-paragraph-long run-on sentence, Ayala Blanco chastises the film as vacuous and simplistic ("a congratulatory laugh for the debauchery of horny guys, a wishful thinking fantasy of empty-headed juniors"); castigates it for repeating the formula set by *Amores Perros* ("shrill plot, *apantallapendejos* [*sic*] pre-Hong Kong rhythm, catchy and invasive soundtrack, anti-psychological hyper-fragmentation, disproportionate advertising"); and censures its failure to live up to the sexual themes of French cinema ("an underdeveloped, complexed, cheap, much-too-late version of *Jules et Jim* without the defiant, hypermisogynistic, vexatious, phallocratic adhesions of *Les Valseuses*").

Unlike García Tsao's disparaging *Beavis and Butthead* reference, Ayala Blanco invokes international media examples to suggest how *Y Tu Mamá También* falls short compared to those other films' artistic achievements. The comparison to *Amores Perros* also prefigures a critical fascination with lumping together several Mexican films of the early 2000s as some sort of "new wave" (Menne 2007) but, as Ayala Blanco's description already illustrates, the connections between these films were mostly paratextual, like the soundtrack or the purportedly "disproportionate" advertisement – and certainly not whatever an "*apantallapendejos* pre-Hong Kong rhythm" is.

His reference to French films demonstrates that Ayala Blanco seems particularly upset at what he deems unimaginative, perhaps even upsetting, sex scenes. He retorts that the supposed "shocking y uncensored [*sic*]" presentation of the films is in fact "hygienic" and "old-fashioned." Later on, he alternatively calls the film a "ero-pedagogic poem" and an "urgent reeducation / de-bestialization / sentimental humanization of unidimensional *machitos*." The review also reads as a play-by-play of the different sexual encounters in the film, name-checking the opening bed scene, the oral sex scene between Tenoch and Luisa, the explicit sexual language during Tenoch and Julio's first fight and during their reconciliation, and the final threesome's morning after.

Nowhere is Ayala Blanco's perverse attachment to the specific sexual imagery in *Y Tu Mamá También* as a way to disparage the film more explicit than in his criticism of the voiceover: "It feels like a squirt of semen in the pool every time the ambient sound disappears and in comes the dreadful voice of the truffautian narrator who, untimely and mechanical, through ineptly written sentences, starts to reveal a bundle of tragic alternate stories, looming misfortunes, and the dark side of things as if summoning a sense of gravity *a huevo*." From the latter part of the sentence, we can gather that Ayala Blanco despises everything about the voiceover: its writing, its delivery, its intrusive interruptions, and its tragic stories. Why, then, begin with the metaphor of semen dripping in the pool? One interpretation: the reviewer thinks the voiceover sullies the aseptic film like the boys' semen does to the pool. But if the rest of the review already suggests the reviewer does not think highly of the film, there cannot be much to sully. A more likely interpretation is that Ayala Blanco compares the aural intrusion of the voiceover to the *sound* of the semen falling into the pool in that one scene. In other words, both instances feel similar on a sonic level: the sound effect of underwater gurgling matching, to the reviewer's ears, the loss of ambient sound during the narrator's voiceover. Perhaps both interpretations have some truth to them. Regardless, the choice to foreground the four-second underwater shot in a critical evaluation of one of the film's most notable formal choices evidences the hold that the film's sexual imagery had on this reviewer.

To reread them now, knowing the international success and enduring popularity of *Y Tu Mamá También*, these two early reviews serve as evidence of some initial critical distaste for the film. Yet, I find them on par with other positive reviews from Mexican critics in how the writers struggle to make sense of explicit sexual content in a mainstream domestic film. For a few supporters, the explicitness and novelty of the sex scenes was a welcome shift to traditional practices in Mexican cinema. For those with more mixed reactions, writing about the sex on screen meant creating an imagined *other* intended audience (teenagers) and speculating about how or why these scenes would be meaningful to that audience. For the film's most ardent detractors, the sex within it was either not liberatory enough, not explicit enough, or not good enough.

Following the release of the film, Jorge Dorantes published another review article in *El Economista* titled "*Y Tu Mamá También*: olvidemos el escándalo" (Let's forget the controversy). In this review, Dorantes offers a guide to examine the artistic qualities of the film without solely focusing on its raunchy elements. He admits that such qualities cannot be observed on an initial viewing because the first time around, "the film will hit your body and emotions directly: there will be laughter, blushing, and perhaps an erection or two." Instead, it is only the second time around, "once the plot holds no more surprises and the buttocks of Gael García and Diego Luna and the breasts of Maribel Verdú have been previously examined," that the subtle details that give the film its humanity will begin to emerge (Dorantes 2001b, 51). Leaving aside the (debatable) assumption that one viewing would be enough to examine the bodies of the protagonists, it is notable that Dorantes doubles down on the film's sexiness as its primary appeal – even a distraction from its other social and artistic contributions.

Perhaps a second (or third) look at the film would allow audiences to engage with elements of the film beyond the sexual content but, for critics and audiences, the sexual content was front and centre when the film was first released. Most importantly, sex was not only a theme in the film that critics either liked or disliked. Sex was *the* structuring rhetorical, conceptual, and thematic form of engagement. From the assessments that teenagers would appreciate the sex scenes, to the personal takes on what its explicit content should or should not be, to the (over)use of sexual figures of speech, sex was an integral part of the critical reception of *Y Tu Mamá También*.

Prestige Sex and Eroticism in International Reception

A key factor shaping the initial local reception of *Y Tu Mamá También* – particularly in contrast to that of *Amores Perros* the year before – was that the former film's trajectory through the international festival circuit occurred *after* its domestic release (Solórzano 2002). After premiering in Mexico during the first week of June 2001, the film did not start showing in international festivals until the end of August. While this timeline meant that the film's festival recognition would not influence its critical success within the national sphere, its domestic commercial success was used as a selling point in its promotion on the festival circuit. Given *Amores Perros*' similarly successful festival run the year before, *Y Tu Mamá También* was heralded as "one of a recent string of successes" that had sparked "what some critics have hailed as a national cinematic renaissance" (Puerta 2001).

Unlike *Amores Perros*, however, *Y Tu Mamá También*'s sexual subject matter was, in fact, not only a key factor for the film's national critical disdain, but also an essential aspect of its marketing strategy and, ultimately, its international success. For starters, the film was the first project developed under Good Machine International's strand of "uncensored cinema," which producing partners James Schamus and Ted Hope started in the early 2000s "to provide financing for quality directors to make risqué movies of their choice under $5 million" (Dunkley 2000, 1). Unwittingly, it also turned out to be *the only film* that could be considered part of this "uncensored cinema" since Good Machine was bought, dismantled, and merged into Focus Features by Universal Studios in 2002 (Harris and DiOrio 2002).

Despite the early advantages of being classified as a risqué project, the official stance from the producers of the film tried to draw attention away from this fact. Producer Jorge Vergara stated that the producing team recommended the film not be watched solely out of morbid curiosity and that, although they could exploit the sexual aspects to their advantage, they had chosen instead to encourage people to go in with an open mind and "be willing to learn something" (Torres 2011, 139). This emphasis on the producers' side to present the film as a serious work rather than purely as an attractive sex flick proves revealing of their greater ambitions for the film, namely its international distribution and recognition.

The film's international festival run was overall successful. At the Venice Film Festival, it won awards for Best Screenplay and Best Newcomers (Smith 2002). The film was scheduled to premiere at the Toronto International Film Festival under its contemporary world cinema program on 11 September 2001, but given the attacks on the World Trade Center towers that morning, it was postponed along with the rest of the events for the day (Kennedy 2012). The film continued its trajectory through different European festivals in late 2001 and early 2002.

The film's positive reception at these international film festivals was soon matched by equally high praise from foreign critics. Critics' organizations across the United States, such as the New York Film Critics Circle, the Chicago Film Critics Association, the Los Angeles Film Critics Association, and the Broadcast Film Critics Association, named it the best foreign film of the year, while the National Society of Film Critics selected it as runner-up for best film of the year. Given the Academy Awards rules, films need to be put forth by the deciding body in their country of origin to be eligible for the best foreign film category. Since the Mexican Academy of Cinematographic Arts and Sciences (AMACC) did not select it as the national candidate, *Y Tu Mamá También* was not eligible for this category. The film was still recognized with a nomination in the Best Original Screenplay category (Gray 2003).

Across its international releases, the film's framing as a sex film only grew. In April 2002, it screened at the 15th Singapore International Film Festival to fully sold-out shows. The already significant expectations for the film were only heightened by the fact that the festival was allowed to screen it without any re-edits, keeping in all the scenes featuring sex and marijuana, which would not be allowed in Singaporean theatres due to censorship restrictions at the time (Jiménez 2002). The same month, *Y Tu Mamá También* was selected as the opening film for an "Erotic Cinema with an Auteur's Vivion" Screening Series in Santiago, Chile, for representing "the highest artistic level" (*El Universal* 2002). Notably, the previous fall Chile had become the most permissive country in Latin America in relation to the film's rating by allowing entry to audiences age fourteen and older. Countries like Argentina, Colombia, Guatemala, and Uruguay followed in Mexico's steps and restricted the film to those eighteen and older, while Bolivia restricted it to twenty-one and older.

Later in 2002, the film began to premiere in countries in East Asia. The poster for the film in South Korea, where it premiered in September 2002, illustrates how its sexual themes transformed in the process of circulating internationally. The most commonly used poster for the film features a medium closeup of the protagonists embracing while floating in a body of water, positioned slightly off-centre. The actors' faces are coloured in a high-contrast yellow-orange, while the rest of the poster (including the water and the title) is coloured in a high-contrast jewel-green and black. When featured internationally, the poster might include a translation into the local script alongside the Spanish-language title.

In contrast, the South Korean poster drastically changes the colour scheme and the sexual dynamics of the protagonists. This poster features a white and sky-blue background that breaks in half the image of the trio dancing and rearranges it so the faces of the boys are clear, but Maribel Verdú is only partially seen in each corner. In the foreground, cut-outs of the two boys on the diving boards while masturbating (their masturbating hands offscreen) create a diagonal strip across the poster. The film's title appears in the centre in white block letters.

The focus on the boys rather than the trio in this poster speaks, in part, to the growing global popularity of the two male leads by 2002. As detailed in chapter 3, the awards and festival attention for the film contributed to the nascent international stardom of Gael García Bernal and Diego Luna. Though it remains unclear whether that was intentional, the South Korean poster also markets the film within the more regionally recognizable "Boys' Love" genre (Kwon 2022). Still, the poster's new colour scheme and reorganization of promotional images sell a markedly different sexual narrative, one where the female object of desire is abstracted, if not erased, and the focus remains on the appeal of the boys' bodies and desires.

Sex as Metaphor in (Anglophone) Scholarly Reception

Following the festival tour and international awards recognition, the home video release of *Y Tu Mamá También* coincided with the beginnings of a movement in the field of film and media studies to think beyond "the nation"

Figure 7
The Japanese poster for *Y Tu Mamá También* follows the same design as
most international posters of the film: the three actors' faces are coloured
in a high-contrast yellow-orange while the water and the film's title are
coloured in a high-contrast jewel-green and black.

Figure 8
The South Korean poster for *Y Tu Mamá También* departs from the
design of other international posters for the film by foregrounding
the two boys and changing the colour scheme.

as analytic and move towards "the transnational." Sensing that the concept of the nation was overdetermining the ways scholars thought about cinema, the "transnational" offered "a subtler means of describing cultural and economic formations that are rarely contained by national boundaries" (Higson 2006, 16). The umbrella of transnational cinema began to function as a shorthand to investigate the global networks of production and distribution that increasingly shaped filmmaking at the turn of the twenty-first century. Soon a plethora of approaches came to be identified as transnational: critical interrogations of the boundaries of national identity within film, regional or continental surveys of film canons, and studies of diasporic and migrant film practices (Higbee and Lim 2010). Though not without its criticisms and detractors, the transnational analytic remained a touchstone of film and media studies scholarship throughout the 2000s and 2010s.

The circulation of these ideas influenced how scholars came to think through *Y Tu Mamá También* and its standing within national and transnational cinema cultures. In one of the most cited articles about the film, Ernesto Acevedo-Muñoz identifies a postmodern generic malleability that, he argues, had overtaken the details and nuances of national topics as regularly treated in Mexican films. Like *Amores Perros*, *Y Tu Mamá También* capitalized on "the lingua franca of contemporary cinema" – which Acevedo-Muñoz understands as violence in the former and sexuality in the latter – to "pass" internationally (2004). For Acevedo-Muñoz, the film represented a continuation and a break: its frank and headfirst approach to sexuality granted *Y Tu Mamá También* "universal appeal" that explained its popularity with audiences beyond Mexico. Despite that universal appeal, the film replicated longstanding trends in Mexican cinema for dealing with gender, class, and national politics.

Other scholars likewise analyzed the film's double address to national and transnational audiences as a result of its mixing of genres. Several scholars would turn to the script's road trip tropes (Oropesa 2008) or the film's documentary style (De la Garza 2009; Finnegan 2007) to analyze how *Y Tu Mamá También* offered a critique of the Mexican nation by contrasting its urban and rural landscapes. In the process, the sexual antics of the film's "teen com-edy" aspects were sidelined, often implicitly relegated to stand in as an ele-ment intended to appeal to mainstream international audiences. For Andrea Noble, the road movie–cum–teen pic side represented the conservative strand of *Y Tu Mamá También*, while its social-realist side allowed it to make a pro-gressive intervention about the effects of economic reform on class and eth-nicity and a reflection on the nation-state in twenty-first-century Mexico. The "trappings of conventional documentary style" deployed in the film served the function of "exposing the human cost of advancing neoliberal re-form" (Noble 2005, 144).

Some scholars read the film as a direct allegory of the Mexican nation in a historical moment of change. For example, María Josefina Saldaña-Portillo uses the ending of the film, when the long-ruling political party PRI has lost the federal elections, as the entry point to reread it as "an allegorical reading of a national allegory" staged "at the very moment of this allegory's historical demise" (2005, 766). For over seventy years, the PRI promoted its right to rule as embodying the interests of the people, and the people voted the party out in 2000. The road trip through the rest of the country in *Y Tu Mamá También* that ends in the protagonists coming back to Mexico City as everything has changed in national politics offers an all-too-perfect synergy of text and con-text. For Saldaña-Portillo, the sexual antics of the boys, particularly their sex with each other in the end, must be read psychoanalytically. "The desire these boys express for each other as substitute father figures," she writes, "reveals the eroticized fulcrum upon which a seventy-year 'ego-ideal' of revolutionary masculinity (PRI papa) turns: the union of PRI/pueblo." This historically in-flected psychoanalytic reading even extends to colonial times: "the positive Oedipal desire expressed by the boys for Luisa, I suggest, expresses a desire for mama España as ego-ideal" (2005, 761).

In her analysis, Elena Lahr-Vivaz (2006) not only interprets the boys' rela-tionship as a potential "radical rewriting of national fables of identity" through a "queering of desire" but also recuperates the film's voice-over as a "virile voice" that is "potent in [its] narrative agency." In stark contrast to Ayala Blanco's comparison of the voice-over to a semen squirt in the pool, Lahr-Vivaz situates this formal feature within a lineage of Mexican nationalist literary tradition wherein a writer's "virile voice" was evaluated based on how it spoke for, and adequately portrayed, the nation. The voice-over narrator's virility, his use of polished Spanish, and – although Lahr-Vivaz does not identify it as such – his implied masculine heterosexuality place him in stark contrast with the sexual and social precociousness of the two male protagonists. This contrast "pries open an alternative discursive space" and prompts Lahr-Vivaz's political reading of the film.

Later readings of the film followed a similar approach of pursuing a queer reading centred on the Tenoch-Julio relationship yet focused on "queering the nation" by situating the relationship as a homosocial bond that reflects US-Mexico cross-cultural influences or examining the film's treatment of gender differences as reminiscent of 1990s New Queer Cinema (Davis 2014; Worrell 2011). For scholars with such approaches, the emphasis on critiquing the status of the nation through their readings of Y Tu Mamá También likewise meant interpreting the road trip and teen comedy sex antics as a form of genre mixing meant for international appeal or turning the sexual elements in the narrative into metaphors for broader historical changes. Scholars proved to be less interested in the specifics of the actual sex in the film than in its thematic and metaphorical resonances.

It was not long before the film became subsumed as part of a larger transnational movement. The continued international success of other Mexican films throughout the 2000s led scholars to think in terms of a cinematic canon that internationalized the nation. The concurrent success of *Amores Perros*, *Y Tu Mamá También*, and *El Laberinto del Fauno* spurred an interest in theorizing a post-NAFTA cinematic sensibility (Hind 2004a) or a "Mexican new wave" (Menne 2007). Likewise, the international popularity and awards success of the "Three Amigos" (Cuarón, Iñárritu, del Toro) briefly defined the work of these three white hetero men directors as emblematic of Mexico's transnational appeal (Carroll 2012). Soon, the idea of cinematic "new transnationalisms" became a continent-wide phenomenon (Tierney 2018). By getting caught in the theorizations of these new waves and international networks, the critical appraisal of *Y Tu Mamá También* became further desexualized. If it was sometimes mentioned in these accounts, the film's sex recedes as merely one data point in the overall "newness" and transnational appeal of the new wave of films.

On its twentieth anniversary, two short monographs on the film brought back to the fore some of its appealing sexual elements. Paul Julian Smith, for instance, opens the first and last of his book's chapters with a brief recounting of the opening and final sex scenes in the film (2022). Meanwhile, in *Mythologies of Youth*, Scott Baugh dedicates two separate chapters to detailing the specificities of the film's sex scenes, not only noting the allegorical, symbolic, and "multifaceted messages" encoded in these scenes, as many other writers have before, but also analyzing the formal construction of key sex scenes (2019, 86). In particular, Baugh illuminates how Luisa's individual sex scenes with Tenoch and Julio are characterized by visual misalignments that reinforce the point where each character is in their narrative trajectory at the moment of the sexual encounter. Both of these contributions are welcome invitations to revisit aspects of the film that first made it stand out and that continue to make it singular in its portrayal of sex as character development.

Chapter 2

Si No Te Hubieras Ido:
Queer Listening to the Youth Soundtrack

Here are the greatest hits of how critics and scholars have characterized the soundtrack of *Y Tu Mamá También*:

- "a compilation of pure congruence ... in sum, the cherry on top of the cake that is *Y Tu Mamá También*" (Franco 2001, 55);
- "the music selection is a scramble, but in this soundtrack there is something for every musical taste" (Naime 2001, 21);
- "Pop songs on the soundtrack are also a plus, striving more for mood than market value" (García Tsao 2001b, 23);
- "Since no road trip is complete without a kilometer-killing sound-track, this pimp-mix disc to Alfonso Cuarón's delightfully mischievous cuming-of-age (skin) flick is most definitely the *boleto*" (Hernandez 2002);
- "evidence of globalized style and production can be found in the film's hybrid soundtrack, incorporating artists as diverse as Frank Zappa, Brian Eno, Natalie Imbruglia, La Revolución de Emiliano Zapata, Flaco Jimenez, and Cafe Tacuba" (Finnegan 2007, 32);
- "the possible second conquest by the United States' culture and language, as demonstrated by Tenoch and the soundtrack, reflects a worrisome element of external colonization" (Hind 2004a, 106).

Despite reviewers' and journalists' early enthusiasm for the film's soundtrack, critical attention to the songs in *Y Tu Mamá También* has waned over the years, becoming a footnote or a quick interpretive afterthought. For most authors writing about the film in the two decades since its release, its songs only warrant a brief mention within a broader description of how it fits within New Mexican Cinema's appeal to global audiences or as a way to reinforce how it borrows from the genre of teen sex comedy. Certainly, the creative decisions for the soundtrack followed in the steps of those set by *Amores Perros* and other Mexican films of the early 2000s, featuring crossover artist collaborations, contemporary re-recordings of older songs, and music in English. But to only consider the soundtrack's song selections as a marketing paratext to the film is to miss the more expansive impact and significance of these selections.

Consider, for instance, the use of the song "Afila el Colmillo" by Titán and La Mala Rodríguez in an early sequence inside Tenoch's house. The sequence begins as the Iturbides' domestic worker, Leodegaria ("Leo"), exits the kitchen and follows her as she walks down the first-floor hallway, up the stairs to the second floor, and into the den where Tenoch is listening to music. The main sonic cue throughout this sequence is the ringing of the phone, which we eventually notice has been next to Tenoch the entire time, yet it is Leo who picks it up, answers the call, and wipes the handset before handing it over to him. The continuous ringing works alongside the four shots' extended duration to emphasize the unacknowledged labour the domestic worker performs for the film's privileged teenage protagonist: not only does she make him a snack that he spits out when he learns who is on the phone, but she also attends to the ringing phone in another storey of the house that he could have more easily answered himself. This short yet poignant sequence offers an early precursor to the widely lauded use of framing, editing, and cinematography in service of representing the labouring life of domestic workers in Cuarón's later film *Roma* (Aguilera Skvirsky 2020; Sánchez Prado 2018). If these visual elements work to draw attention to Leo, the song functions as an aural reminder of Tenoch's contrasting privilege. As Leo approaches the second-storey den, the song becomes louder, matching the level of the phone ringing and eventually overpowering Leo's own voice when she answers the phone. Tenoch only lowers the volume of his music when he wants to be able to hear Luisa on the other side of the call. Later in the film we learn more about Leo: when the trio drives past a sign for Tepelmeme, the narrator informs us that this was her hometown and sheds some light on Leo and Tenoch's relationship. But Leo never really gets screentime to speak for herself, a stark distinction from the much-debated attempt to "let the subaltern speak" in Cuarón's later Spanish-language film. The song in this scene, instead, gestures to how the presence of the ruling class (as a character or a filmmaker) acts as a sonic disturbance that prevents us from dwelling on the inner lives of others around them.

Notably, the part of "Afila el Colmillo" most clearly heard in the scene is the song's sampling of another song, the 1960s tropical music hit by Mike Laure "Tiburón a la Vista." The 2001 remix takes Laure's catchy refrain "Tiburón, Tiburón" and overlays it on top of a number of synth effects, which accentuate the sonic force of the song as Leo approaches its source. By blasting his music, Tenoch takes up space throughout the house. By the time the scene cuts to the shot inside the den, the song's volume and sound effects make the music the centre of attention. If only for a few seconds, we are immersed in its catchy beats, seduced by the sonic symbols of Tenoch's leisure – when only moments before, we witnessed the invisibilized labour that sustains it. As an individual recording, "Afila el Colmillo" fits the bill for the type of remix that was the signature of the Y Tu Mamá También soundtrack by taking a popular recording from the past and adding more contemporary pop elements to it – indeed, this segment of the song plays on repeat over the menu on the film's first DVD release. Considering it within the context of the film itself offers an even better understanding of how the recording's remixing operates at multiple levels, from characterization to scene composition to spectatorial affect.

Figures 9–12
Leo walking through the Iturbide house while Tenoch's music blasts.

In this chapter, I propose we revisit *Y Tu Mamá También* through its song selections to examine a number of important aspects of the film's queer legacy. First, a look at the initial promotion of the soundtrack based on youth punk rock bands reveals a sharp contrast with the eventual impact the film would have on the rediscovery and popularity of other, more traditional music genres. In the absence of a score, the songs provide the template for the narrative's emotional trip, suggesting that looming future tragedies coexist with the pleasures of the present. I analyze this musical template as a queer form of understanding time within the film's diegesis akin to what scholar Elizabeth Freeman calls "temporal drag." Finally, no re-evaluation of the musical legacy of *Y Tu Mamá También* would be complete without a consideration of the iconic song "Si No Te Hubieras Ido," its role in the film's final cantina scene, and its sudden and enduring popularity.

A Truly Bilingual Soundtrack

The resurgence of *rock en español* and the arrival of music videos in the late 1980s, along with the rise of teen telenovelas and music-themed reality TV shows in the early 1990s, dictated that most of the films in Mexico during this decade – of which a significant portion was aimed at the teen market – used popular songs and its young stars as promotion to reel in crowds (Torres San Martín 2011, 157). As Mexican critic and filmmaker Karla Paulina Sánchez Barajas explains, for *Amores Perros*, *Y Tu Mamá También*, and other Mexican films at the turn of the twenty-first century, "rock music went from being a leitmotiv to an integral part of the film's soundtrack precisely because of rock's potential to enrich cinematographic language" (2016, 15). Producers became interested in the creation of musical atmospheres that would intensify not only the plot but also the characters' – and the viewers' – psychological experience.

A key element in the success of these late 1990s to early 2000s commercial films rested on a strategic use of the film soundtrack, given that placing a successful single into MTV and radio rotations provided free publicity and a way to bring into the theatre audiences who lacked an interest or pre-existing investment in Mexican cinema. *Amores Perros* had a two-disc sound-track that included not only tracks featured in the movie but a set of songs "inspired by" it, mimicking a marketing strategy common among Hollywood films of the past twenty-five years. The impact of the soundtrack extended beyond the strategy of placing a single on MTV: it adopted the language of alternative music to define the film's tone in relation to the cultural taste and ethos of Mexican middle-class audiences, who were very familiar with this kind of music. According to Ignacio Sánchez Prado (2014), these strategies made *Amores Perros* a mediatic product without precedent in the Mexican cultural market.

The soundtrack for *Y Tu Mamá También* also followed in the footsteps of its predecessor by featuring all songs played in the film and displaying a heavy dose of alternative, crossover artists. The tracks on the record included new songs and covers of older classics, bringing several decades of Mexican music together. The soundtrack was released with a special DVD that in-cluded several music videos (Torres San Martín 2016). In her audience re-search on the film, Patricia Torres San Martín (2011) notes that after its release, a majority of young Mexicans immediately bought the soundtrack and the pirated video, and then acquired the DVD as soon as it was released. Still, Cuarón regularly emphasized in interviews the filmmakers' intent to appeal to a wide range of age groups, claiming that in addition to his own music tastes, his then-teenage son Jonás also advised on the music selections (Leon 2001). The soundtrack achieved moderate success, achieving Gold cer-tification in Mexico and receiving a nomination for "Best Compilation Soundtrack Album for Motion Pictures, Television or Other Visual Media" at the 2003 Grammys.

Besides the variety of Mexican artists, the soundtrack also featured artists from across the Anglophone music world. In his review of the soundtrack, critic Mauricio Hammer described its transnational character as such: "Take a guess, cine-spectator: in what unthinkable place, in what obscure point of the universe can you find Frank Zappa and Marco Antonio Solís, La Revolución de Emiliano Zapata and 'La Sirenita' (which Rigo Tovar used to sing), Brian Eno and Bran Van 3000. Easy: in the twenty-first-century Mexican postmodernity, which reproduces without restraint a bi-national culture that fuses language, customs, and traditions on both sides of a 2000-kilometer border ... *Y Tu Mamá También*, the soundtrack for the new, controversial film by Alfonso Cuarón, is overwhelming proof of this" (2001, 45). Hammer goes on to describe the record's track listing by identifying the artists' various national affiliations: "the King of Tex-Mex, Flaco Jiménez"; "the Swede by accident but *gringuísimo*[1] by vocation Eagle Eye Cherry"; "the Australian Natalie Imbruglia." This transnational aspect of the soundtrack was by design: a way both to generate excitement for the soundtrack (and in turn, the film) and to instigate news coverage focused on the eclecticism of the song selection. The record producers contributed to this attention in the news by emphasizing the underdog status of the soundtrack that matched the film's own maverick success in securing independent financing. In particular, music producer Carlos Lara claimed that transnational record companies thought of the soundtrack as "too crazy, alternative, and risky an idea that was not commercially viable," and hence it had to be made "independently, with the initiative of only a few people, and with the creation of a new record label: Suave Records" (Rock 2003, 6).

Producers also drew considerable attention to their labour of curation and to the turmoil they went through to acquire the rights to all the songs. According to Lara, some artists turned down the offer to contribute to the sound-

---

1 *Gringo* is a colloquial expression in Mexican Spanish to refer to US nationals. The superlative in this case implies something akin to "*gringo* to the bone."

track because of their opposition to the film's content: alternative pop artist Beck considered the film "offensive," while rapper Snoop Dogg claimed to be uninterested in "a film that tackled homosexuality" (Castillo 2001). In several interviews, producers celebrated the positive response from Frank Zappa's widow Gail when she saw the film and granted the rights to include "Watermelon in Easter Hay" – a song that the Cuarón brothers claim to have been listening to on repeat while writing the script. Alfonso Cuarón even claimed that, when he showed the film to Gail Zappa, she stated, "If Frank were alive he would be proud to be a part of the film" (Caballero 2001).

The first single of the soundtrack was "Here Comes the Mayo," a collaboration between the Mexican punk rock band Molotov and the English electronic music band Dub Pistols. Early coverage of the film's music tended to emphasize the fact that the Mexican band took time off their sabbatical to contribute to the album.

The music video for "Here Comes the Mayo" was released over a week before the premiere of Y Tu Mamá También in Mexican theatres, and therefore functioned as a promotional video spot for the film (Garcia 2001). Interspersed with actual clips from the film, the music video's narrative concerns the two bands seemingly recutting the film in a theatre projection booth. Members of the supporting cast (including Diana Bracho, who plays the film's titular mother and is explicitly referenced in the song lyrics) sit in the movie theatre watching the screen until they realize the disturbance and join the artists in the projection booth. The collective dance in the tight projection booth offers visual allusions to a rave or even a sex party, including the song's signature move of shaking a fist above one's head in a back-and-forth movement to match with the lyric "Shake my macana mama / Shake, shake my macana" (macana meaning baton or club).

"Here Comes the Mayo" features verses in both Spanish and English along with a Spanglish chorus consisting of the song's title (an allusion to being close to ejaculation) and the repeated phrase "Shake my macana mama / Shake, shake my macana." It is not surprising that most of the lyrics reference explicit sex acts and macho posturing, but there is a distinct inflection on the contexts of these sex acts between the two languages: while the lyrics in English sung by the Dub Pistols suggest one man having sex with one or more women, the lyrics in Spanish sung by Molotov allude to more diverse sexual contexts implying varying degrees of homosociality. For instance, the song starts with metaphors for threesomes ("sandwich de cuates" [friend sandwich]) that imply the third person is another male friend ("Mal movimiento y te llueven mecates" [one false move and you're struck with ropes]). Later, the initiation of another threesome is even more direct: "Le hablo al tocayo, se saca otro gallo" (I call my buddy, he pulls out another cock).

While it is unclear whether both bands had seen the film before writing the lyrics to the song or how much they knew about the plot, these references in the Spanish lyrics seem to be alluding to the famous threesome at the end of the film, a fact that would not have been obvious to audiences when the song first came out. Still, I would not give too much credit to Molotov for choosing to weave homosocial ambiguity into their lyrics, especially considering that the band is best known for insistently doubling down and ignoring critiques of their homophobic song "Puto" for decades (Fabian 2013).

In retrospect, the initial focus on these alternative rock artists has proven to be a less significant part of the legacy of the soundtrack. Following the release of the film, popular attention quickly shifted to Marco Antonio Solís's song "Si No Te Hubieras Ido," which plays over the cantina celebration scene near the end. By the time the film premiered in London in spring 2002, there were reports that theatres would play "Si No Te Hubieras Ido" during the pre-show (Hoy 2002). In the two decades thereafter, the musical legacy of the film would be inextricably tied to the international success of Solís's hit ballad.

Sonic Disruptions and the Drag of Time

Because *Y Tu Mamá También* has no accompanying score, its two main aural features are the extradiegetic narrator's voiceover, provided by actor Daniel Giménez Cacho, and the diegetic songs. As explored in chapter 1, initial critical responses to the voiceover were negative (Ayala Blanco 2001), but this formal feature has received considerably more attention in scholarly writings of the film ever since (Chung 2011; Lahr-Vivaz 2006). As for the soundtrack, while its intended alternative rock appeal is evident within the film during the scenes set in Mexico City, there is more to it than this predetermined marketing value. The use of music in film can serve multiple purposes: "to help realize the meaning of a film"; to "make potent through music the film's dramatic and emotional value"; to "support, accentuate, to be auxiliary to the visual image" (Dickinson 2008, 16). The song selections in the film contribute to its queer sensibility for all of these purposes.

In his book, Paul Julian Smith calls the soundtrack selection "improbable" and more characteristic of the (then fortyish-year-old) filmmakers than the young characters in the film's diegesis (2022, 65). In contrast, I argue for analyzing this contrapuntal use of music and narrative as an opportunity to think about the music on the same level as the voiceover – offering us a distinct layer of storytelling even though the songs purportedly come from the characters' own battery-operated player. For Carlos Monsiváis (2006, 514), music in new Mexican cinema of the early aughts acted as "a central protagonist" that set "the affective space from which [these films'] portraits of life emerged." Following Monsiváis's insight, I propose relistening to *Y Tu Mamá También* by paying closer attention to how the song choices set this affective space throughout the road trip sections and to the ways the songs' interruptions foreshadow the film's end, namely the demise of the boys' relationship and the death of Luisa.

In a rare instance of close analysis of the film's soundtrack, Scott L. Baugh (2020) proposes reading the musical composition of Frank Zappa's "Watermelon in Easter Hay" to understand the aesthetic structure of the film given the Cuaróns' claim that they listened to that song on repeat while writing the script. The "(post)structurally experimental qualities" of Zappa's music resonate with the "exceptionally convoluted soundtrack" of *Y Tu Mamá También*, "intermingling subtle but distinct volumetric and contrapuntal qualities and visuals" (Baugh 2020, 26). While I am sympathetic to this reading, the ultimate interpretation misses a key element of how the *non*-rock music selections operate in the film: by facilitating turning points whose temporal and spatial disjunctions are not merely formalist but unmissably affective. In short, the musical choices illustrate not only the film's poststructuralist play but also its melodramatic intensities – therein lies part of the film's queer legacy.

Tracing the musical selections of the film and contrasting them to the final song, with its representative shift in genre and tone, reveals a texturally and affectively different queer reading from how critics and scholars have engaged with it so far. The kind of *queer listening* I propose is inspired by scholar Elizabeth Freeman's notion of temporal drag. Borrowing the concept of drag, a practice central to queer theory's critique of the gender binary, Freeman proposes to reconsider "drag" as a temporal phenomenon (2010). Like the way performance drag interrogates purportedly stark gender distinctions, *temporal drag* questions the supposed stable divisions of time. Temporal drag refers to the way that a person might reenact, in displaced form, events that she could not give meaning to at the time they occurred. Temporal drag points to the influence of retrogression, delay, and the pull of the past on the experience of the present.

As Hye Jean Chung (2011) argues, the film's voice-over already acts as an *acousmêtre* that invokes other times and other spaces through sound, thereby destabilizing the ideological assumption of unity within the film's diegesis. Whenever the voice-over narrator brings up events that happen before or after the scenes depicted onscreen, he "dissolves the demarcation between past, present, and future" by implying that "different temporalities always coexist on parallel planes" rather than "progressing in one direction in a chronological trajectory" (Chung 2011, 110). The acousmatic voice of the voice-over expands temporally beyond the diegetic space presented in the film and thereby transforms the protagonists' journey across the Mexican rural landscape into a traversal through time. By focusing on the other significant sonic element in the film (the songs), I extend Chung's argument beyond the realm of narrative. The temporal drag offered by queer listening concerns not only the internal lives of the characters or the chronotropic dimensions of the space they inhabit but also the viewers' experience of the film. Listening closely to the film's use of songs reveals how sound and image work contrapuntally to present the merging of alternative temporalities and divergent affects.

While the visual contrasts in *Y Tu Mamá También* bring together a story about teenage sexual awakenings with footage of rural Mexico to provide a critique of the nation, the sonic contrasts in the film bring together sexual talk with sounds of loss to accentuate a queer perspective on mourning and the atemporality of sexual and sentimental connections. For instance: discussing a beloved deceased former lover, as Luisa does in one scene, not only brings back the memories of their sexual escapades but also surfaces Luisa's own sense of imminent death. The film acknowledges both of these sentiments, the past and the future one, through the music playing in the background during Luisa's retelling, a barely perceptible song lamenting the loss of a love and the desolation left in its wake.

Listening to the soundtrack of *Y Tu Mamá También* as a source of temporal drag is a queer perspective on the film not merely in the sense of queer as in "disrupt" or "odd" but of queer as in "pervert." Attending closely to the merging of song choices with visual cues within specific scenes in the film points us to moments where the irruption of death – as in the demise of a character, the end of a relationship, or the conclusion of the music itself – is interwoven with the opening up of the main characters' sexual horizons.

The following three instances of song use and interruption occur sequentially during the road trip portion of the film, leading up to the moment when the protagonists arrive at the motel where Luisa's seduction of Tenoch will disrupt the amicable tenor of their journey. To some extent, these songs – "Cold Air" by Natalie Imbruglia, "By This River" by Brian Eno, and "La Tumba Será El Final" by Flaco Jimenez and Freddie Ojeda – underscore the focus of the characters' conversations (or lack thereof) in the scene they appear in. The appearance and disappearance of these three songs also signal a sonic disruption in the narrative – a record scratch, if you will – whether through a sudden end to the song, the conversation, or the car's engine. These interruptions mark not only a break with comedic and/or dramatic effects but also an instance of temporal drag, a moment where either the past or the future interrupt the experience of the present.

Following the encounter with the quinceañera fundraiser, the song "Cold Air" by Australian pop singer Natalie Imbruglia begins playing over two extreme long shots of the station wagon cruising through the winding roads of the rural highway. In the first shot, the car emerges from behind a hill and approaches the camera, while, in the second shot, the car drives right to left across the frame. There are no other vehicles on the road in either of these shots, visually enforcing the notion that the protagonists are in a world of their own – even if only for these forty seconds of real time. Aurally, the volume of the dialogue varies depending on the proximity of the car to the camera position, but the volume of the song remains constant, suggesting its thematic status as extradiegetic despite purportedly coming from the boombox inside the vehicle. Once the film cuts to the medium shot from the hood of the car, the dialogue and music rise as we watch the three protagonists centred in frame.

Throughout the sequence, the boys ask Luisa about any sexual experiences she had before meeting her husband. She recounts meeting and falling in love with her high school boyfriend, her first time having sex, and missing classes to have more clandestine hookups with him. Luisa speaks wistfully

Figures 13–14

Two long shots of the rural landscape with only the station wagon cruising on the road: first driving towards the camera and then driving across the screen, as seen while Natalie Imbruglia's "Cold Air" plays on the soundtrack.

of him, describing his leather jacket and motorcycle and recalling their plans to move to Côte d'Azur with the excitement she might have had at the time. The boys' light-hearted teasing of Luisa about the youthful sexcapades ends abruptly when she matter-of-factly mentions that the boyfriend died in a motorcycle accident.

The focus on learning about Luisa's backstory and the higher volume of the dialogue draw attention away from "Cold Air" until the last moments in the scene, when all the characters fall quiet and we hear Imbruglia singing "air" in an extended syllable. Yet even if the lyrics of the song remain mostly unintelligible throughout the sequence, the melody and the singer's voice underscore the melancholic tone of the story and prefigure the retelling of loss that will end the exchange. Characterized as a whisper by critic X. Andrés Naime (2001), Imbruglia's singing in this tune carries through feelings of emptiness and longing, feelings that reverberate with the shots of the deserted highway, the mention of the boyfriend's death, and finally, the interruption of the narrator to include another story of past tragedy: the truck accident that left two people and countless hens dead on that highway ten years earlier.

Following this interruption by the narrator, "By This River" by British ambient music artist Brian Eno begins to play, offering an even more straightforward song about loss and mourning. With sparse verses and melodic electric keyboard, the song uses lyrical repetition to paint a musical picture of a stagnant relationship coming to an end. The lyrics themselves emphasize the temporal drag of the relationship being finished before its purported end: "You talk to me / As if from a distance / And I reply / With impressions chosen from another time, time, time." Much like its title, the song's words, though few, are heavy on water metaphors, evoking rain, rivers, and oceans. First seeming a stark contrast to the arid drylands the characters drive on at that moment, these metaphors signal the promised ocean destination.

The song plays over two long takes. The first one captures the station wagon from the side of the road as it drives past a group of kids playing soccer on a dirt field. The second one captures the side of the road from the per-

Figures 15–17 *Above and following page*
Scenes of rural Mexico's everyday life as seen from the window of the station
wagon while Brian Eno's "By This River" plays on the soundtrack.

spective of the station wagon's windows: different kinds of trees, empty fields,
lone animals grazing, small houses with corrugated metal roofs, gray concrete
buildings with no exterior coat of paint, and people walking.

Notably, "By This River" is one of the few songs during the road trip that
the main characters do not talk over. There is no dialogue to distract from
the montage between the visuals and the music. The audience, like the characters, sits in silence for almost a minute, watching the scene of the rural quo-
tidian landscape and listening to Eno's song – that is, until the song begins to
skip and then stops altogether. Julio interjects with "No, *güey*, that's a great
song," to which Tenoch replies that the CD player from which they have been
playing their music has run out of battery mid-song.

After this incident, the characters are faced with having to turn on the radio
for musical accompaniment for the rest of their trip. Diegetically, this change

breaks the insulation created by the fact that the characters listening to their curated music selection isolates them from the scenes around them. Formally, the shift disrupts the contrapuntal montages of English-language melodic songs with the landscapes of rural Mexico. The film's song choices moving forward from this moment in the narrative tend towards more examples of Mexican traditional music.

Because of this shift, the next song to play on the soundtrack is "La Tumba Será El Final" by renowned Tejano musician Flaco Jimenez. Lyrically, the song represents a stark contrast with Imbruglia's "Cold Air" and Eno's "By This River": rather than alluding to a lost relationship, Jimenez's song instead promises undying devotion to the loved one. The song plays on the radio as the characters make their way through more populated areas around the highway, stopping mid-road to let a herd of cattle cross, and driving past federal police arresting a group of farmworkers. These shots are shorter and intercut with several shots of the trio inside the car. The contrapuntal editing here no longer pairs an English-language moody tune with long takes of the Mexican rural landscape. Instead, the heartfelt love song promising eternal commitment "until the final grave" contrasts with the dialogue, especially the boys describing the different ways they have sex with their (and, as we later find out, each other's) girlfriends.

As Luisa probes their answers about what exactly they do with their sexual partners, the boys reveal their inexperience by first awkwardly, then unimaginatively, describing their sexual acts. To the boys' claim that they do "everything," Luisa asks about slowly inserting a finger into their partner's ass. The mention of ass takes the boys by surprise and they exclaim "Culo?!" in unison as the car breaks down. The humour in the juxtaposition of the boys' shock and the vehicle's breakdown becomes all the more emphatic for viewers familiar with the song and the anti-social strand of queer theory, namely the work of scholar Leo Bersani. Bringing together the lyrics "the grave is the end" with the characters' discussion of sticking a finger in your partner's ass makes a sonic pun of Bersani's famous provocation that "if the rectum is a grave in which the masculine ideal [...] of proud subjectivity is buried, then it should be celebrated for its very potential for death" (1987, 222). Notably, the song keeps going on the radio as they step out of the vehicle and notice the extent of the smoke coming out of the hood. The sequence ends.

The Cantina Song, Revisited

"Si No Te Hubieras Ido" (If you had never left) is the last song heard in the film itself and, in many ways, its appearance encapsulates the temporal drag the soundtrack has been building up to throughout the film.

Written by Mexican singer-songwriter Marco Antonio Solís in 1983, "Si No Te Hubieras Ido" was first recorded by singer Marisela and included on her album *Sin Él*, which was produced by Solís in 1984. The song was released as a single and became very successful in Mexico. Solís re-recorded the track to include it on his 1999 album *Trozos de Mi Alma*, a collection of songs written by him but previously recorded by several other performers. This newer recording, with its updated nineties sound mix, is the version featured in *Y Tu Mamá También* and in the movie's soundtrack. The single was not only the film's main hit song but also a top-ten smash for Solís, playing on Mexican national radio for weeks and peaking at number four on the *Billboard* Hot Latin Tracks chart in the United States (Torres San Martín 2011, 158).

The newfound transnational and cross-class popularity of the single contributed to record label Fonovisa's decision to re-release *Trozos de Mi Alma* only a few years after its original release. In an artist profile in *Billboard* about this renewed popularity in the United States, Marco Antonio Solís called "Si No Te Hubieras Ido" one of his "fortunate songs" (Cobo 2004, 77). Over the next two decades, covers of the single would be recorded by several luminaries of the Hispanophone music industry, including bands like Maná, Moderatto, and Reik and solo artists like Juan Luis Guerra, David Bisbal, Charlie Cruz, and Yuridia – one of the few recent covers by a female vocalist. At the film's sixteenth-anniversary retrospective during the Morelia International Film

Festival, Solís admitted, "From then on, with that song, my career took an international turn" (2017).

While Solís had long been a popular idol for working-class publics, Carlos Lara recalls that, after its appearance in *Y Tu Mamá También*, the song started showing up in social events frequented by "people from Polanco and Las Lomas," two of the wealthiest neighbourhoods in Mexico City (Rock 2003). As scholar Dorian Lugo Bertrán argues, in a film soundtrack characterized by alternative rock and ambient songs, the inclusion of Solís's ballad is "striking and glorious at the same time" since it had long stood as the epitome of *música popular* (music for the masses). Its newfound popularity among wealthy elites who used to disdain música popular "consecrates [and] baptizes clandestine love" for the formerly scorned music genre as if revealing deep down "an unconfessed intrigue, a 'third party' of any sex or sexual orientation" (Bertrán 2009). This sexually ambiguous intrigue echoes the themes of the film and may account for the crossover popularity of the song.

Concurrent with the film's release, the musical theme likewise became an anthem for Mexican youth at the time (Torres San Martín 2011). It was embraced in high-class bars and nightclubs across Mexico, where the preferred musical genres were Anglophone pop and electronic music. In fact, the song was taken up in very much the same way that it is portrayed in the film: played in bars at the end of the night for youths to drunkenly lament something lost even in the moment of celebration. The powerful containment of current euphoria and future loss carried the song (and its singer) from being staples of música popular to playing in the city's posh neighbourhoods, across the country's youth-targeted venues, and into the Anglophone world.

During a promotional interview for *Y Tu Mamá También* in 2001, reporter Magaly León asked the film's creators how they decided to include "Si No Te Hubieras Ido" in the bar scene. Producer Jorge Vergara offers a cryptic yet effusive answer: "It was superb! I am convinced that [Solís] wrote the song for the film and for Maribel [Verdú] without knowing it." Although the filmmakers tried to have Solís write an original song for the film and considered others among his repertoire, none could beat the emotional impact of "Si No Te Hubieras Ido." "That was the perfect song, it transforms into a *canción cachondísima* [a super horny tune]," concluded Vergara (León 2001).

Fifteen years later, co-writer Carlos Cuarón offered a different origin story for how this song came to be in this scene: Mexican photographer Maya Goded was working on her exhibition *Sexoservidoras*, a series of twenty photographs of sex workers posing in their regular places of work. Goded encouraged her subjects to feel at ease while they prepared for their photoshoots and, while interviewing one of them at a cantina, noticed that the sex worker stood up and played the Marco Antonio Solís song on the jukebox. Based on the simplicity of that moment, Goded suggested the song to Alfonso Cuarón. "We listened to it," Carlos Cuarón recalls, "and thought there could be no other song for that scene" (FICM 2017).

Despite their differences, both explanations for why "Si No Te Hubieras Ido" was selected as the song for the final cantina scene point us to what makes this scene work. Cuarón's anecdote helps make sense of the song's synergy with its setting. The simplest explanation is that the sex worker just liked the song and decided to play it on the jukebox, but the enduring legacy of the film's scene and the song's eventual crossover popularity prompt us to imagine otherwise. So I suggest that we must understand the sex worker's decision to get up and play the song while she was being interviewed in a cantina as a kind of vernacular instinct about the setting's sonic registers. Her familiarity with the place speaks to an implicit bodily knowledge about how a song like "Si No Te Hubieras Ido" mirrors and shapes the confluences of space and time in a cantina.

Why does the cantina matter? The cantina is generally defined as a musical space of neighbourhood sociality. It is emblematic of "low-life" musical venues that, in conjunction with the musical styles usually played there, register a working-class blight, or culture *de abajo* (from below). As Deborah Vargas argues, the popular status of the cantina frames the transgression of class and sexual mores: "the source of economic abjection to a neighborhood's perspective of itself as a family barrio" and "a site of gender/sexual abjection often violently policed by parameters of gender and sexual normativity" (2013, 65). Traditionally, the cantina space is where heteronormative masculinity plays out in rigid normative registers of gender and sexuality, symbolized by the patronage of single men and heterosexual coupling for sale.

In its cinematic lives, the cantina perpetuates this heteronormativity yet enables the momentary, fantastical reprieve from it as well. Mexican classical films from the mid-twentieth century with famous actor-singers like Pedro Infante and Jorge Negrete would often feature drunken singing interludes where the male protagonists laid bare their feelings and insecurities. As Sergio de la Mora points out, the musical interludes – the melody in these classical melodramas – functioned as a utopian space for the expression of male intimacy: "homosocial practices and expressions are central to the construction and stylization of Mexican masculinities. In these films male homosocial bonds are reconfigured and strengthened in cantinas or cabarets through musical performance, functioning as the privileged space and the discursive modality through which singular, bounded, and fixed notions of heterosexual masculinity are simultaneously challenged, modified, and reinscribed" (de la Mora 2006, 71). For writer Carlos Monsiváis, the cantina was "the limit of experience," an archetypal locale for suffering in Mexican popular culture that offered a place where "the male character was forged and his psychic collapse plotted, fatal resolutions were made, and songs became edicts of self-destruction" (1995, 118).

"Si No Te Hubieras Ido" proves to be a quintessential cantina song because its lyrics seamlessly fit within this affective structure. From its opening line, "Te extraño más que nunca y no sé qué hacer" (I miss you more than ever and I don't know what to do), to the start of the chorus, "No hay nada más difícil que vivir sin ti" (There is nothing more difficult than living without you), the song is filled with superlatives expressing an immense loss and the emotional devastation from missing the addressee of the song. But the lyrics also contain a sense of indeterminacy that leaves open-ended both the first person singing and the "you" being addressed. The song allows for the external expression of loss to hide a different internal subject of longing. In *Y Tu Mamá También*, such ambiguity is further deployed as a prelude to and anthem for the protagonists' climactic coming together, prompting what de la Mora once described as "song, humor, and liquor enlisted to facilitate the expression of emotionally charged, and potentially gender-transgressive, declarations of true and unfailing friendship" (2006, 90).

The film's cantina scene by the beach re-imagines the previously latent homoeroticism of the "drunken men singing" trope. Whereas earlier films featured men singing to each other about women, the disembodied voice of Marco Antonio Solís and the indeterminate *tú* (you) of the song's address abstract the man-on-man desire of the setting, which the film then literalizes in its narrative. The song playing in this scene offers another instance of a temporal drag, with the past, classical traditions of Mexican cinema inflecting the present-day setting and the modern cinematographic style of the scene. Throughout, the cantina remains the place where repressed desires and frustrated aspirations become unspooled.

Buddy movies in both Mexican and Hollywood cinemas have often contained the potentially disruptive homosocial bond with women characters acting as a heterosexualizing ploy that elicits, while at the same time diffusing, the otherwise inexpressible declaration of the male couple's commitment to and love for each other. The treatment of these female characters can often cross into misogyny when the women are imaged as threatening and disruptive to the male bond. Circulating as sexual objects, these women characters exist merely to underscore the men's heterosexuality, and their roles are marginal to the male-male relationship (de la Mora 2006, 88).

In *Y Tu Mamá También*, Luisa does exhibit some of the characteristics of the woman character presented as a ploy in a male buddy movie. She completes the boys' sexual journey (and their psychic journey) by being the facilitator for the eruption of their implicit homoeroticism. In the cantina, she literally dances between them, offering an erotic mediator and lowering the barriers between them. Their threesome represents the boys' ultimate submission to their shared affection and therefore the ultimate transgression of the masculine code they have championed and have failed to honour as machos. Still, Luisa explicitly calls out the boys' immaturity and continually embodies more self-assurance. Her willingness "to be more fluid in her interactions" as the journey progresses illustrates her "emancipation from external markers of self-validation" (Worrell 2011, 163).

Whatever the shortcomings of Luisa's presentation elsewhere in the film, the cantina scene sidesteps any such reductive characterization. As Jorge Vergara enthusiastically put it, the cantina scene in the film indeed transforms a melancholy romantic ballad into a *canción cachondísima*, a super horny song, because of Maribel Verdú. This horned-up transformation comes from the merging of the opening chords of the song and the long shot of Luisa dancing to the camera as she walks from the jukebox back to the table. Her staring straight into the camera captures the viewer's attention, folding them into the tune of the song before Solís's vocals kick in. Like in the case of "By This River" earlier in the film, this is one of the few moments where the main characters do not speak over the diegetic music and the background sound fades out. The song's instrumentation performs the narrative and emotional functions of a musical score. The electric guitar intro, in particular, offers the aural cue to match and accentuate Verdú's sensual self-referential dancing. If one thinks about it too long, it does not make sense: Solís's crooning refers to loss and sadness, yet every other aspect of the film turns the musical arrangement into a ballad for pleasure.

Looking back at this scene knowing what will unfold, Luisa's commanding stare into the camera reveals her not only as determined to bed the two young men at once, but also as resolute to live out the rest of her days on this beach. She might be looking at her immediate sexual conquests and looking ahead to her remaining days – and sees both with a similar sense of anticipatory desire. "Si No Te Hubieras Ido" now points us to a moment when Luisa will no longer be there, a fact that the film has regularly hinted at but not yet revealed.

The vaunted and insidious *tú* that is gone certainly refers to Luisa, but also gone are the imaginaries that the two male friends had of each other, of their friendship, and of their own sense of self. As Dorian Lugo Bertrán suggests, the *tú* was always already gone, but the event instigated by the song is the moment where "the lack becomes evident" so much so that "the 'I' is no longer victorious nor self-sufficient" (2009, 60). The death of such narcissistic jouissance becomes the birth of responsive desire.

Even more starkly, the introduction of this song presents the moment Luisa takes control of the film herself. The camera approaches her as the instrumental opening begins, her back still to us as she dances sideways to the tune. Luisa then turns around and stares directly at the camera just as Solís's voice comes on. *Te extraño más que nunca y no sé qué hacer.* She then begins dancing towards the camera, forcing it to retreat and keep pace with her. It is significant that Luisa remains in the centre of the frame in a medium close-up throughout this retreat back to the table: the camera once called "straying" (Noble 2005), "wandering" (Acevedo-Muñoz 2004), and "distracted" (Barbas-Rhoden 2019) now proves to be abiding, on course, and intensely focused on the woman protagonist. Luisa finishes her tequila shot and breaks eye contact with the camera to focus on the two young men. She pulls them up and directs them to dance next to her as the song begins to swell into its chorus. *No hay nada más difícil que vivir sin ti.* For those familiar with "Si No Te Hubieras Ido," Luisa's taking control of this scene is not only visual but also aural. Like with other songs earlier in the narrative, the film presents it as music coming from within the diegetic world, namely the jukebox, but the song's original recording has been clearly edited to fit the scene. The instrumental introduction is cut short, and Solís's first verse comes in as soon as Luisa turns around to face the camera. The second verse is also left out so that the beginning of the chorus matches the moment Luisa gets both boys to dance alongside her. The impact of the scene lies in its seamless orchestration of visuals and sound, punctuated by the realist aesthetics of Lubezki's camerawork and the affective resonance of Solís's vocals. But this moment of the scene ultimately belongs to Luisa: determined, commanding, radiating. Maribel Verdú simultaneously plays her character's resolve, desire, and jouissance all at once in just seventy-five seconds.

Once again, it is significant that this scene plays out in a makeshift cantina space. The cantina, as Deborah Vargas proposes, is a chronotrope, a slowing down of space and time distinct from normative temporality, one that forges other spatial dimensions of possibility, potential, and promise. "The markers of time in the space of the cantina keep the pasts ongoing: in the furniture that is never replaced but held together by electrical tape, in the stage space that is never remodeled, in the acoustic technology that is never updated" (2013, 61). The cantina also warps time through its happenings: it represents a space of congregation for its many customers who want to exist outside of normative time, even if momentarily.

Time drags in the cantina space. These chronotropic spaces therefore encapsulate not only a latent queerness in the homosocial relationships of the patrons but also temporal drag created by a sense of suspended animation that brings together disjunctive temporalities. In *Y Tu Mamá También*, music, setting, and narrative converge to produce such queer temporal drag. The song lyrics about loss prefigure the film's denouement when Luisa dies of cancer and the two male friends stop seeing each other forever. Yet this foreshadowing occurs in an instance of celebration, in the midst of a *borrachera*, and in the moments before the three protagonists engage in an ecstatic three-some. The temporal disjunction held by the song operates as a queer structure-of-feeling, containing at once both the passion of the near future and the tragedy of the distant one.

The song is an affective "working out" of that which is lost at a moment when it is not yet lost, but it is in the process of being lost. The moment may present itself as a celebration precisely because that loss is not yet here, or because its coming is a welcome reprieve. For a film very much interested in the reworking of classical tropes and emblematic of new media cultural formations in the decades to come, the climactic scene appropriately *queers time*

Figures 18–19
Luisa stares directly at the camera, seducing the audience, as "Si No Te Hubieras Ido" starts to play on the jukebox.

Figure 20
The trio engages in the initial foreplay of their sexual encounter in the left
foreground of the frame while the right background reveals the traditional
sense of the cantina as a space for homosocial camaraderie.

– its disjuncture between song and narrative presents us with an emotionally
charged moment of suspension. Gesturing at what will be lost yet figuring
this loss as a potential celebration, the characters' dance to "Si No Te Hubieras
Ido" holds the past, present, and future suspended in time, if only for a brief
ecstatic moment.

There is likely no other song in *Y Tu Mamá También* that is better remembered than "Si No Te Hubieras Ido," even if the specificities of the lyrics are
not familiar to non-Spanish-speaking audiences. How we arrived at this state
of affairs is indeed a marker of the film's queer legacy insofar as it signals a
perversion of the original aims of the soundtrack. The intent to appeal to a
youth market's music tastes, important to the early promotion of the film,

has not left as lasting an imprint on the sonic reception of the film today. The abrasiveness (lyrically and sonically) of "Here Comes the Mayo" is long gone from the popular memory of the film and has been replaced by the melodic melancholy of Solís's crooning. As I detail in the conclusion, fan-created media about the film take their cue from the latter song by pairing their remixed film fragments with sentimental tunes. In that sense, the legacy of queer listening to *Y Tu Mamá También* carries on.

Chapter 3

White Briefs, Uncut Dicks, and Green Eyes:
Theorizing Mexican Masculinities

As I explained in the introduction, the conceptual framework laid out by Octavio Paz in *El Laberinto de la Soledad* figures the construction of Mexican masculinity as a competition predicated on chingar (fucking and fucking over) one's fellow man. For Paz, Mexican men engage in a constant defensive struggle to keep themselves closed, to prevent vulnerability, by avoiding *rajarse* (being open, vulnerable, or penetrable). One asserts one's masculinity by forcing others to make themselves vulnerable: a man seeks to chingar his rival and make himself *el gran chingón*, and his rival *el chingado*, symbolically penetrated and feminized. That original framework and its various reworkings by other scholars across the decades has long proven generative for the analysis of the sexual and gender politics of *Y Tu Mamá También*.

Instead of revisiting this well-worn terrain, I propose building on the understanding of masculinity as homosocial and hypersexualized – a consistent refrain from Paz's original theorization through its later reformulations – to think through a different thread: the ambivalent pleasures of the Mexican male body as simultaneously a sign of masculinity, an object of desire, and, increasingly, a representational blank slate for international consumption. As Héctor Domínguez-Ruvalcaba reminds us, "if virility is prestigious [and] effeminacy is dishonorable" in the construction of machismo as through sexual domination, then "the male body claims its centrality as the hero figure," yet "this centrality makes his body an object of desire" (2007, 65). How Mexican cinema presents the masculine body vacillates between these poles: showcasing virility and negotiating desire. For the classical films of the Mexican Golden Age, for instance, that meant exalting the epitomes of virility as sexually desirable macho figures while desexualizing those men who did not embody such virility, often by relegating them to comedy genres.

The place of *Y Tu Mamá También* in this history is significant. The film's invitation to desire with, yet simultaneously lampoon, its male protagonists continues to contend with the macho paradox of Mexican masculinity. The sex scenes are imbued with a sense of comedy, often at the expense of the male characters and their sexual inadequacy, thereby thwarting the expectation that these men are the epitomes of virility. Yet the film undoubtedly became the springboard for its male stars' international success, due in large part to how the actors were objectified and promoted as examples of new millennial forms of masculinity. At the same time, the film stands as a turning point in the unabashed depiction of naked male bodies in Mexican media productions, whose implications reach back to the mid-twentieth century and continue to resonate two decades into the twenty-first century. It is because of this complex set of negotiations, I propose, that the film holds a privileged place in the queer cinematic figurations of Mexican masculinities.

This chapter explores the class, ethnic, and queer politics of masculinity in and beyond *Y Tu Mamá También* by attending to the mediation of the film's two men protagonists (and the actors that play them) within the film itself, in contrast to other films before and after it, and throughout press coverage of the actors in the decade following the film's release. Examining how these two men's bodies are aestheticized, fetishized, and later re-signified signals specific inflection points where Mexican masculinity is reframed and transformed.

White Briefs, or Watching the Mexican Man's Body Onscreen

The epilogue of Sergio de la Mora's 2009 monograph *Cinemachismo*, an investigation of masculinities across Mexican film history, dwells on the (then) emerging international star persona of Gael García Bernal. De la Mora muses that "Garcia Bernal looks equally beautiful and authentic playing a sexy and vulnerable young man straddling a motorcycle and speeding past awe-inspiring landscapes" as he does "playing a flirty fledgling writer of pulp screenplays who slips out of a pool in tight, wet, white briefs, revealing just enough to make his fans pant" (2009, 166). By the time de la Mora wrote of García Bernal's multifaceted attractiveness, the actor's star persona had become fully internationalized, relying on an "ethnic stardom" (Tierney et al. 2017) that allowed him to play a plethora of Latin American nationalities for US and European productions. It is significant that de la Mora ends his study with a gesture to García Bernal's unique star persona because it was already clear by then that the actor's international appeal signalled new forms of embodying Mexican masculinity.

In particular, the form of Mexican masculinity that García Bernal and Diego Luna – together and separately – came to represent in the decades after *Y Tu Mamá También* posed a notable departure from the long-standing ideals that de la Mora's work examines, ideals best personified by the star of the classical Mexican cinema era of the 1950s: Pedro Infante. Infante "embodied the collective hopes and dreams of Mexico's popular sector" and earned the special recognition of being called *el hijo del pueblo* (the people's son). His working-class origins contributed greatly to the authenticity with which he portrayed charming and long-suffering migrant working-class men from northern Mexico. Throughout his film career, Infante often portrayed the "Mexican common man who is driven by his passions, be they related to the family in general, mother figures in particular, drinking, and hanging out with his buddies" (de la Mora 2009, 70).

Infante represented both symbolically and physically the ideal of the Mexican man. He was known for his highly publicized exercise routines and for constantly showing off his perfectly toned body (Corliss 2007). Before his contemporaries in classic Hollywood, the Mexican actor regularly went topless in his films, proudly displaying his bulky muscularity in everything from shower scenes to fight scenes. According to Anne Rubenstein, the obsession with Infante relates to his embodiment of "moral and physical perfection as well as national pride" as well as his personification of ideal models of masculinity that include the urban charro, the sentimental macho, and the working-class common man. By bringing these different facets together, "Infante represents a living vision of what it might mean to be Mexican" (2001, 126).

Following the success of *Y Tu Mamá También*, the mainstream press in Mexico tried to pursue a comparison between the classic and the millennial stars, a strategy that would continue as the internationalization of its male leads increased over the years (de la Torriente 2001; Huerta 2009). De la Mora rightly contests these comparisons, calling them "a stretch of the imagination," by noting how Infante's working-class roots and his appeal to ordinary Mexicans alone differentiate him from the distinctly middle-class appeal of both García Bernal and Luna (2009, 167).

While the star personas of these Mexican male actors half a century apart are hardly comparable, I still contend that *Y Tu Mamá También* does extend and contest the tradition set up by Pedro Infante's films in the use of buddy comedy tropes and the focus on the bodies of its male stars. De la Mora himself analyzes how, like in Infante's buddy movies, *Y Tu Mamá También* uses the narrative device of an erotic triangulation in which a woman enables men to express their homoerotic desire, yet the latter film "asks audiences to acknowledge pan-sexuality and the complexities of desire; it challenges homophobic audiences; unabashedly brings out and embraces head-on the homoerotic impulses barely repressed in Pedro Infante's classic buddy movies of the '50s" (2009, 176–7).

Consider the film *¿Qué te ha dado esa mujer?* (1951), about two male transit officers (Pedro Infante as Pedro and actor Luis Aguilar as Luis) whose friendship is tested when one man's girlfriend confesses her love for the other one. As roommates, the two men share a one-bedroom suite where they each have a single bed. Like many of Infante's films, this one features multiple opportunities to display the actor in various stages of undress. In one scene, for instance, despite the men running late for work, Pedro springs up and runs to the shower, where he proceeds to perform a rendition of one of his songs. Later, in a screwball comedy sequence, one of the female love interests gets trapped inside the men's suite and hides their pyjamas. Upon stripping down to their white boxers and realizing their pyjamas are gone, Pedro states, "Oh well, guess we'll sleep in our birthday suits." The men bend over to strip themselves of their underwear but stop just as they hear the woman hiding behind a couch.

In these scenes, the male bodies are on display, yet the display is playful. It is a sign of the bond of the men's friendship while also a showcase for the audience's amusement. The men's naked presentation implies virility, and sexual appeal without sexuality. Indeed, their shared bedroom does not carry any affective undertones until later in the film, when it becomes a place of longing: after their personal drift over the woman that came between them, Luis listens to the radio in the room while Pedro listens to the same song in a cantina. The shared musical cue leads to a spectral appearance of Pedro in the bedroom as the two friends duet a song about lost friendships.

Given the use of the shared bedroom as the place for fraternal camaraderie and suppressed homosocial longing in *¿Qué te ha dado esa mujer?*, I cannot help but think of these scenes when watching the first verbal fight between Tenoch and Julio in the motel bedroom in *Y Tu Mamá También*, which occurs entirely while Julio lies on his bed in his white briefs while Tenoch berates him. Unlike in the aforementioned fifties screwball comedy, the bedroom here is the site of conflict, not friendship or longing. In the latter film, only

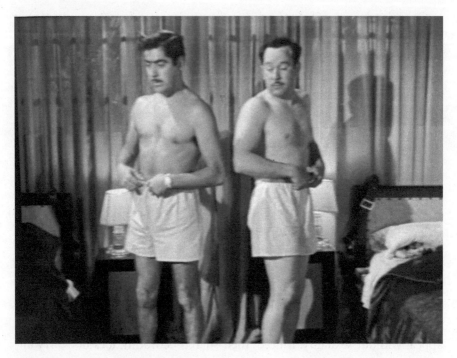

Figures 21–22 *Above and opposite*
Pedro Infante and Luis Aguilar prepare to strip down from their white boxers
when they suddenly hear a noise in *¿Qué te ha dado esa mujer?*

one of the two men is in his underwear, a constant reminder of his sexual de-
sirability that creates a further strain when Tenoch wants to know everything
about how and when his girlfriend had sex with Julio.

Instead of white boxers, however, Julio wears white briefs. We have seen
him wear these before, at his apartment when Tenoch calls him to mention
Luisa's acceding to taking the road trip to Boca del Cielo. These briefs are a
deliberate character feature for Julio, especially given that we never get to ob-
serve Tenoch's underwear in this much detail; he is more likely to be fully

naked. (Though we do get a brief look at the latter's gray briefs – with no elastic band and no noticeable brand name – when Luisa pulls down his pants during the climactic threesome scene, arguably that piece of clothing is not foremost in anyone's mind during that moment.)

In the annotated published version of the *Y Tu Mamá También* script, two footnotes draw attention to Julio's briefs. During the apartment scene, the first footnote reads, "It took hours to convince Gael to wear Rinbros briefs" – with no explanation of whether the resistance was to wearing briefs in general or those white briefs in particular. During the motel fighting scene, the second footnote emphasizes the return of the briefs by noting how this wardrobe choice differed both from the boxers listed in the first draft of the screenplay and from the shorts that García Bernal supposedly wanted to wear instead (Cuarón and Cuarón 2001, 115, 198). The decision to name the brand of the white briefs speaks to the specificity of the wardrobe to the character and the setting: Rinbros has been a Mexican no-frills brand for men's underwear since at least the mid-twentieth century. In contrast to the overtly aestheticized Calvin Klein white briefs popularized by Tom Hintnaus in the 1980s – or their successor, the boxer briefs worn by Mark Wahlberg in the 1990s (Cole 2012) – fitting García Bernal with white Rinbros briefs emphasizes the underwear's matter-of-factness for the character. Julio sleeps in these because they are the affordable modest variety he wears every day.

It is crucial, then, to trace how the motel fight scene resignifies the connotation of these white briefs by doting them with an unmissable erotic charge. While Tenoch remains fully clothed and mostly in the dark, Julio lies almost naked in full display on the bed with the warm light of the nightstand contouring his toned body. The visual dynamic reinforces the relative position each young man has within the argument: Tenoch attempts to come out of the darkness of not knowing about the cheating going on behind his back while Julio exposes himself by sharing (editorialized) details of the sexual encounter with Tenoch's girlfriend. Through this blocking, the scene also recasts Julio's undergarments into a prop that entices and eroticizes the man's body. As writer Manuel Betancourt suggests, white briefs are enticing because of what they do to the male body: with their "perfect thigh-to-bulge ratio ... briefs titillate by the very shape they contour and convey" (2023, 115). Unlike their matter-of-fact appearance in the apartment scene, in the motel confrontation scene the white briefs appear tighter, closely contouring the borderline between García Bernal's butt and thigh and teasing the crotch area just barely obscured by his raised leg.

The erstwhile "welcome mundanity" of the white briefs acquires a newfound charge during this motel room scene, at once suggesting "a bland ideal of masculinity" and "eroticiz[ing it] in delightfully unintentional ways" (Betancourt 2023, 116). Barely sitting up on the bed, Julio's tightened abs are all the more visible given the shadow contrast from the single source of light

Figures 23–24
Julio walking around wearing white briefs in his apartment.

Figures 25–26
During their argument, Julio's relaxed pose while wearing only white briefs
reinforces the sexual upper hand he presents over Tenoch.

from the nightstand. Though the white briefs cover the fact of Julio's (uncircumcised) penis, they still titillate by suggesting its hidden appeal and prowess. Tenoch has seen Julio naked numerous times before – in the shower at the country club he even mocks his friend's uncircumcised penis. But after learning of the transgression, Tenoch witnesses Julio's sexual appeal anew. Despite the sense of confrontation, this scene also signals the beginning of the affective turning point in the boys' relationship that will lead to consummation in the final threesome.

The exposed bodies of Mexican men in cinema mean not only a display of manliness but also their configuration as embodied sexual beings. In the motel room scene, the way Gael García Bernal is warmly lit, and always in a relaxed pose, while wearing white briefs, offers new matrices for envisioning the appeal of the millennial Mexican man. The film's focus on the male body as a site of sexual appeal, however, stops short of framing these bodies as objects to be looked at, a feature that is best illustrated by considering the penis. In contrast to the sensual appeal of García Bernal lying in his white briefs or the passionate kissing between both actors in the final sex scene, during the actors' full-frontal naked scenes, the film undermines, or at least refracts, an objectifying gaze. Their penises are not necessarily objects of sexual desire but rather comedic props, character backstories, and paratextual anecdotes.

Uncut Dicks, or the Class Politics of Male Nudity

While the film itself allows only a few brief glances at them, the main characters' penises peppered media discussions of Y Tu Mamá También at the time of its release and in the decades since. In particular, mentions of the penis prosthetic that Diego Luna had to wear to match his character's circumcision showed up in interviews about and reviews of the film. While one reviewer noted that "Luna *gamely* wears a prosthetic glans" (Smith 2002), Luna is quoted in another article saying, "With a prosthetic penis, I felt I was

Figures 27
Gael García Bernal framed in profile wearing only white briefs, warmly lit, abs
tightened, during the first fight between the boys in the motel.

dressed: it wasn't my dick" (Feinstein 2002). The prosthetic is also brought
up in the official film paratexts, including the Cuaróns' annotated script and
the DVD commentary by Luna, García Bernal, and Andrés Almeida. In the
latter, Luna further complains that the prosthetic's non-stretch material caged
his own engorging penis during the first sex scene between Tenoch and Luisa.

The repeated mentions of Luna's prosthetic underline a constant in *Y Tu
Mamá También*'s representation of its two men protagonists' bodies: the talk
about genitalia far surpasses their visual depiction. During the road trip conversations, the protagonists discuss penis size and blow job techniques, draw
attention to involuntary erections, and comment on the appeal of foreskin
(or lack thereof). When Luisa first asks Tenoch to drop his towel and mas-
turbate in front of her, she tells him that his penis leans left, not right as he
had previously claimed. The audience learns a lot about the young men's

penises through these lines of dialogue. It is only during the shower scene at the country club that the audience might actually catch a glimpse of said penises. Yet these glimpses are not accidental; once again, *the dialogue* in the scene offers the most information, focusing squarely on the anatomical differences between the friends.

In this shower scene, Tenoch insults Julio's uncircumcised penis by comparing it to a monk's hood (in the original Spanish) or a deflated balloon (in the English subtitle translation). These metaphorical differences remind us how foreskin can act as a floating signifier, taking on a series of meanings depending on the context. For Harri Kalha (2014, 382), "the preputial semiosphere manifests its essential flexibility, as modern foreskin fantasies run the associative gamut from the down-home rural to urban modernity, where foreskin explicitly plays on the symbolic of ethnic and social transgression," especially when the intended audience of a piece of media is imagined firstly as white and upper-middle-class. From the perspective of popular US media, for instance, the foreskin is, at best, a fetish marked as "very European" or, at worst, a racist code for immigrants' uncivilized practices (Allan 2019). The geopolitical differences that inform the "preputial semiposphere" surface during the road trip when Tenoch once again brings up Julio's foreskin as a sign of the latter's ugly penis. In this moment, however, Luisa's positive response ("Qué rico!") signals her more open, worldly sensibility and the specificity of Tenoch's perspective on aesthetic valuations of penis anatomy.

Namely, the differences in the boys' penises represent yet another opportunity for the film to portray the characters' class differences. Unlike in the United States, circumcision is not commonly performed in Mexico; parents must explicitly request the procedure.[1] Barring religious or cultural tradition

---

1 According to reports from the World Health Organization, the lowest rates of male circumcision are found in Europe, Latin America, and southern Africa. Within the US, rates for Latino men are significantly lower than for any other racial or ethnic demographic (Kowalski and Nowak 2016).

(and there is no indication that the Iturbides are of Jewish descent, for instance), it may be implied that Tenoch's circumcision stands as a symbol for his family's aspiration to US-style practices. Like Tenoch lifting the toilet seat with his foot at Julio's apartment and at the low-rent motel or Julio spitting on the car window, the film uses these details to draw attention to the social and political dimensions of its protagonists' bodies. Their deployment as character symbols and as paratextual talking points nonetheless pushes a redefinition of how onscreen Mexican masculinity could be presented, discussed, and evaluated.

For all the critical interest in comparing the realist aesthetics of *Y Tu Mamá También* with those of *Roma*, Cuarón's next famous film set in Mexico, little has been said about the contrast between the depictions of full male nudity in both films. The latter film only has one such scene: the film's central character, housekeeper Cleo (Yalitza Aparicio), and her romantic interest Fermín (Jorge Antonio Guerrero) skip their plans to see a movie and have sex in a hotel room. Afterward, the young man wordlessly retreats to the bathroom, removes the shower rod, and proceeds to execute an elaborate kung fu routine of parries and thrusts with the pole.

The explicit nakedness of actor Jorge Antonio Guerrero in this scene struck critics in different ways. One critic described it as "timeless, in the same way female nudity is sometimes used as a link to millennia of human art" (Yoshida 2018), while another characterized it as a "display of raw machismo and jangling man junk" that felt "incongruously violent, random, yet still somehow sensual" (Lee 2018). For scholar Robert Irwin, the scene was "unprecedented in showcasing indigenous male eroticism" (Lilley, Aviles, and Castillo 2019).

The focus on the significance or timelessness of this scene derives, in part, from the fact that it is *Roma*'s only scene of male nudity, yet such attention also results from the framing and blocking of the scene. The fixed camera position presents us with Guerrero's naked body for several minutes in a front-facing tableau: this is full-frontal nudity that demands to be simultaneously

Figures 28–29
Tenoch and Julio comparing penises and playing around in the showers at the
country club.

Figures 30–32
Depicted in centre frame in high definition, Jorge Antonio Guerrero's naked body
in *Roma* is presented in a way that demands being gazed at and confronted.

gazed at and confronted. The detachment with which critics approached the scene, whether by celebrating its art-like timelessness or reacting to its supposed rawness, belies the fact that the film encourages dwelling on the bare male body long enough to consider its appeal and its repulsion.

In visualizing the physicality of a Mexican working-class man, Guerrero's naked body and kung fu moves share more in common with Infante's various topless appearances than with García Bernal and Luna's scenes. Still, the male nudity in *Roma* serves as a foil to look back at the presentation of the naked male protagonists in *Y Tu Mamá También*. For one, it emphasizes how the latter film offers penises in a variety of presentation styles, from the matter-of-factness of the early sex scenes to the playful comedy of the country club shower scene. *Roma* also subtly albeit explicitly reinforces the class dynamics Cuarón codifies in his characters' genitalia. While Guerrero has previously been cast as the Indigenous character foil to famous Mexican white protagonists (Llamas-Rodriguez 2023), his uncircumcised penis in *Roma* stands to remind us of Tenoch's class-tinged mockery in *Y Tu Mamá También*.

Although Gael García Bernal and Diego Luna spend far more screen time naked in their film, it never presents them as objects to be gazed at and scrutinized. That is not to say that there cannot be a perverse fascination with catching glimpses of the flopping penises as the boys are running around the showers or swimming in the dirty pool; it is, rather, that these glimpses are furtive, not absorptive. The realist aesthetic of the film discourages becoming engrossed in these bodies. The obsession with the bodies and the sex appeal of the *actors*, however, became a source of much media attention following the release of the film, and has continued to shade how we look back at the depictions of masculinity in *Y Tu Mamá También*.

Figures 33–34
While the wide shots encourage admiring their naked bodies, the glimpses at García Bernal's and Luna's penises in the underwater scenes are furtive at best.

Green Eyes, or the International Sex Appeal of the White Mexican Man

Even if the film stops short of objectifying its male stars in its full-frontal scenes, the response to the film only contributed to the sexualization of the two actors' star personas. Julio and Tenoch are sexually inexperienced teens nakedly prancing around, but Gael and Diego quickly became magnetic actors adored for their mature sex appeal across the world. Soon after they were jointly awarded the Premio Marcello Mastroianni at the Venice International Film Festival, the Mexican newspaper *Reforma* ran a comparative profile of the two actors' rising celebrity status. The profile writers characterize García Bernal as "a visceral actor ... all guts, few words, expressing everything with his eyes" while Luna stands as "a dreamy actor" (Rangel, Cabrera, and Huerta 2001). As their star personas grew throughout the first decade of the twenty-first century, the mainstream attention to their bodies and sex appeal was incessant. Food metaphors, body synecdoches, and other (hit or miss) bons mots plagued their profiles in the national and international press in the years thereafter.

For example, in the aptly titled 2003 article "Nude Wave" in *Film Ireland*, writer Annick Coelmont credits García Bernal's "Gaelicious nudity" for driving the success of the string of the three Mexican films he had recently starred in: *Amores Perros*, *Y Tu Mamá También*, and *El Crimen del Padre Amaro*. His international move in the next couple of years – including another iconic white briefs scene in Pedro Almodóvar's *La Mala Educación* (2004) – garnered García Bernal titles like "SexMex" and a "cinematic animal" and comparisons to deceased US male stars like James Dean, River Phoenix, and Marlon Brando (Leal 2004; Reyes 2004; Rousselot 2004; Segoviano 2004). By 2005, his profile in *Vanity Fair*'s "Hollywood Portfolio" section was accompanied by the title "The Hot Tamale" and an opening line that characterizes him as a "bundle of intensity and *muy caliente* looks [who] has arrived as a new leading man for the global-cinema age" (Smith 2005, 380). Besides its groan-inducing cultural tokenism, the "hot tamale" moniker remains grossly inadequate: tamales are doughy and plump, the opposite of the lean, toned physique García Bernal would sport by then.

Meanwhile, Diego Luna's boyish looks sparked a different set of comparisons, more teen heartthrob than classic cinema star. For instance, Luna brushed aside being called "the Mexican Leonardo DiCaprio" when reports first appeared about his filming *Y Tu Mamá También* (Mendoza de Lira 2000). Hagiographic reports about the actor compared his nascent heartthrob persona with family-sourced anecdotes about his nickname growing up being "diegordito" – a portmanteau combining his name with the Spanish term for chubby (Huerta and Cabrera 2004). Though he was set to promote new film projects, the two profiles of Diego Luna in *Interview* magazine during the mid-2000s spend almost half their questions recounting the appeal and experience of *Y Tu Mamá También*, reinforcing the idea that the exposure from this film was directly linked to the sex appeal the actor now conveyed in the magazine spread. A letter to the editor responding to Diego Luna's photoshoot for the *Interview*'s February 2003 issue states:

> Dear Interview,
> Wow! Bruce Weber's sizzling photos of actor Diego Luna dramatically reconfirmed something for me – I am soooooo gay. Gorgeous! Thank you!
> MATTHEW B., Los Angeles, CA

Luna's homosexual appeal would reemerge when he played Harvey Milk's lover in Gus Van Sant's *Milk* (2008), but the inordinate focus on their sex appeal quickly became a burden for both actors. In 2004, García Bernal admitted to the French newspaper *Liberation* that "being the sex ambassador of Mexico is a very funny thing and a heavy responsibility. I am both horrified and very proud of it" (Rousselot 2004). By 2007, in a dual interview for the Mexican magazine *Proceso*, both actors lamented the loss of privacy and heightened scrutiny brought about by their celebrity status.

Corroborating the popularity of García Bernal's and Luna's naked scenes from *Y Tu Mamá También* on pornographic websites such as AZnude.com, scholar Paul Julian Smith demonstrates that "twenty years later, they are still remembered by connoisseurs of youthful male bodies" (2022, 37). That early legacy remains unparalleled, even if nowadays more Mexican actors can be seen naked in film and television productions for international consumption. If we consider only those productions created for the streaming platform Netflix, there is Alfonso Herrera in *Sense8* (2015–18), Luis Gerardo Méndez in *Club de Cuervos* (2015–19), Diego Calva in *Desenfrenadas* (2020), Diego Boneta in *Luis Miguel: La Serie* (2018–21), and Eugenio Siller in *¿Quién Mató a Sara?* (2021–22).

A key aspect that unites these emerging and established Mexican actors with international recognition is the fact that they are all light-skinned. For García Bernal, the mainstream press was always at pains to draw attention back to his green eyes, calling them "green eyes that speak volumes" (Rangel, Cabrera, and Huerta 2001), "beautiful, expressive light green eyes" (Segoviano 2004), "green eyes that change colour with the light" (Rousselot 2004). After *Y Tu Mamá También*, his star "iconicity" relied on the fact that he was able "to shed his Mexican markers of identity in order to become an empty signifier, both culturally and ethnically, that may be filled with a wide array of national and postnational cultural meanings" (Sánchez Prado 2013, 153). According to Ignacio Sánchez Prado, García Bernal's ability to become this "empty icon, whose symbolic value lies not in his specific Mexican origin, but on his trans-Hispanic performances," lay in his ability to shed the markers of both Mexicanness and masculinity previously constructed around his body. That ethnic and sexual flexibility that fuelled the international rise to fame for the two *Y Tu Mamá También* actors has also been a feature of the crossover career paths for other Mexican actors after them.

Far from embodying "what it might mean to be Mexican" from a working-class perspective, as Infante and his contemporaries once did, these new Mexican actors are international starlets first. Their light skin and colourful eyes have allowed them to easily move in and out of playing different nationalities and ethnicities for transnational appeal. Indeed, García Bernal expressed a desire to "see [himself] as Latin American first ... because feeling Latin American implies celebrating differences and absurdities shared across the continent" (Lopez 2006). The cinematic image of the Mexican man transforms into a blank slate for international consumption.

The ways of figuring Mexican masculinities in, and since, *Y Tu Mamá También* are multiple and overlapping. While engendering new forms of depicting male bodies in comedic, playful, and intimate ways, the film also turns the physical characteristics of these bodies into symbols for class and sexual status. The scenes of male sexuality, sometimes awkward and other times sensual, remain more character-driven than gratuitous, despite the arguments of the film's critics and censors. The sexualization of the actors following the film's success nonetheless proved to have longer-lasting effects on the perception of Mexican actors on the international stage.

If *Y Tu Mamá También* represented a turning point in the cinematic mediation of Mexican masculinity at the time of its release, its afterlives through new media platforms have further allowed audiences to re-encounter forms of desire within the narrative and on the queer remembrances of its sexual moments while, at the same time, imbuing them with a different affective force. The conclusion traces these afterlives by focusing on the legacy of the film's most famous kiss.

Conclusion
The Media Afterlives of a Famous Kiss

No account of the queer classic status of *Y Tu Mamá También* could exist without accounting for the legacy of the kiss between Tenoch and Julio. Mexican scholar Patricia Torres San Martín best encapsulates the scene's enduring significance when she explains that it marked simultaneously the success of and backlash to the film: "the bewilderment, the nervousness, the silence and the laughter, as well as the censorship and devastating criticism, granted *Y Tu Mamá También* its lasting popularity" (2016). In her book-length analysis of young viewers' reactions to the film, Torres San Martín documents the charged yet ambivalent responses these early audiences had to this moment. One respondent attempted to describe his feelings by saying, "as a man, one finds a lot of meaning about friendship, and what love means, and how confused we are … and about masculinity … but just because there are some similarities [with the film's protagonists] does that mean that … you're homosexual or that you want to be with a close friend." Another, more articulate respondent summarized the scene's impact as such: "I saw the movie with a long-time friend … and throughout the movie we were laughing like, *güey*, *güey*, remember when we pulled something like that? Then the scene with the kiss happened and we were left, like … we got out of the movie theater and we sat for like fifteen minutes without speaking, just thinking about our own masculinities" (Torres San Martín 2011, 184, 186).

But it was not only young Mexican spectators who had complicated feel-ings about the scene. Ten years after the film's release, Carlos Cuarón still vividly remembered that, at its premiere in Mexico City, people cursed and whistled when Tenoch and Julio kissed. During the premiere, a gay theatre and film director who was friends with Cuarón reportedly said, "Thank you for showing clearly the image of the Mexican macho for the first time: Julio and Tenoch kissing" (quoted in Aguilar 2021). Meanwhile, scholar Sergio de la Mora recalls attending two public screenings around 2001 and 2002: one in a multiplex on Paseo de la Reforma in Mexico City on the film's opening day, the other in a multiplex at a large shopping mall in Sacramento, Califor-nia. At both screenings, de la Mora remembers that large segments of the au-diences reacted "vocally with visceral disgust" to the sight of García Bernal and Luna kissing passionately. "The visual spectacle of men kissing," de la Mora suggests, "clearly registers anxieties regarding what is deemed to be in-appropriate behavior between men" – or at least, what was inappropriate at the time (2009, 176). Echoing Carlos Cuarón's anecdote, de la Mora's experi-ences indicate that popular sentiments around masculinity, particularly Mex-ican masculinity, shaded the initial reception of the kiss between the two male protagonists.

The queer media legacy of the film can be traced as a short media history of this (in)famous moment, from these initial audience responses, to the film-makers' struggles to keep the scene uncensored for home release distribution, to the kiss's resurgence in fragmentary forms through user-generated online content, and finally to the ensconcing of the scene as *the* defining moment of the film as evidenced by more recent retrospectives of the film. In 2013, Diego Luna expressed to *Al Jazeera* his amusement at "the amount of talk that that kiss has provoked" (Frost 2013). Little did he know it would continue to amuse and beguile audiences for another decade after that.

Back in 2002, the then infamous kiss was one of the film's three nomina-tions at the MTV Movie Awards Latin America in the category of Mejor Beso (Best Kiss). Given that the appeal of the MTV Movie Awards had always been its "self-effacing fun" and "irreverent categories" (Reinstein 2022), it was not surprising that *Y Tu Mamá También* won Película de la Gente (Favourite Film) that year and that each of its protagonists' pairings received a nomination for Best Kiss. Even that an instance of two men kissing was nominated in this category was not unusual: the same year, the more gay-panicky kiss between Jason Biggs and Sean William Scott from *American Pie 2* won the category at the US MTV Movie Awards. In retrospect, perhaps the most surprising part is that the winner in the category was Maribel Verdú's kiss with Diego Luna rather than either of the two involving Gael García Bernal.

The MTV Movie Awards' self-effacing irreverence aside, the threesome scene, along with several of the film's other sex scenes, faced significant pushback from international distributors. In her analysis of the making of the R-rated version of the film, Caetlin Benson-Allott (2009) notes that the filmmakers had to accede to MGM's demand for a "family-friendly video version" of the film "in order to secure *any* US distribution." Cut from the film were segments of Tenoch's sex with his girlfriend, the entire scene of Julio and his girlfriend, and any frame that included the boys' penises. By "sanitizing" the film through these edits, Benson-Allott concludes, the US video distribution made *Y Tu Mamá También* "the subject of the same transnational neoliberal forces that it seeks to critique" (2009). Losing the climactic threesome scene near the end, in particular, was not only an artistic impoverishment of the film but also a muddling of its political and social critique.

The threesome scene is cut short at the moment when Luisa sits on Julio's lap while facing Tenoch. This edit removes the moment when Luisa stands between the boys and then kneels down, disappearing from the frame. It also removes the entire thirty seconds of Tenoch and Julio standing naked next to each other and their subsequent intimate kissing moment. Beyond undermining much of the texture of the film by deleting several minutes' worth of sex scenes, erasing the moment when the boys embrace and kiss also disrupts the narrative by making the emotional punch of the denouement baffling and unearned. Absent the climax that brings the two boys together, their disgust

Figure 35
The famous Tenoch-Julio kiss.

and alienation the morning after comes off as an overreaction that cheapens the end of the film.

Years later, those who first watched the film's US release on video are still surprised by the existence of these omissions. In the summer of 2023, for instance, a Twitter user called out Blockbuster for only renting out the censored version of *Y Tu Mamá También*: "when I rented 'y tu mama tambien' from you, you had edited out all the gay content and I didn't know why their friendship got awkward." This prompted a viral response from other Twitter users who found themselves newly making sense of their memory of the film and what they once considered a strangely incoherent set of final scenes. "I've been wondering for years why it was so lauded when it seemed slightly disjointed to me," stated one user. "I have a crazy story about watching that movie [in] college and now some dots are connecting," tweeted writer Saeed Jones.

While reflecting on having to create an R-rated standard edition at MGM's behest, Alfonso Cuarón later lamented that he "castrated [his] movie" (Hirschberg 2003), an ironic metaphor because, if anything, the Tenoch-Julio kiss stands as *Y Tu Mamá También*'s most widely disseminated media progeny. Despite the initial attempts at censorship, and some of those early negative reactions from audiences, popular estimation for this pivotal moment has only grown more positive. During the apex of listicle writing on the internet, the threesome and the boys' kiss would regularly show up among the rankings for "hottest movie sex scenes" and "best onscreen kiss" in mainstream international venues like *Vogue Japan*. In a fifteen-year retrospective, US culture writer Joe Reid (2017) claimed the final threesome was "still the hottest 3-way sex scene in movie history" and described his personal experience watching the two boys kiss as such: "The moment itself plays in slow motion, with the guys inching closer to each other, giving the audience a moment to consider just how fraught and sexual their friendship has always been. Up until the last second, you *still* expect them to get interrupted. And then they don't. It is at the same time a symbolic representation of their characters (their closeness made physical) and also a moment of base, horny desire. A brilliantly tender piece of character work and also *wildly* hot. It's the rare scene that feels both transgressive and utterly necessary."

For those of us too young to watch the film in theatres at the time of its release, the significance of the kiss has grown out of networked, if not collective, modes of reception. Namely, the surge of fan-created film paratexts with the rise of social media platforms in the 2010s has solidified and transformed the appeal of this scene and *Y Tu Mamá También* in general. Looking for "intertexts [that] offer valuable evidence for the contemporary reception of a film that is now two decades old via digital platforms that did not exist on its first release," Paul Julian Smith considers the clip reels of the film on the popular database site IMDb and a grid of GIFs on the collating site Giphy. Smith calls the former a "studied cinephilia" that "attempts to condense a diverse oeuvre into artistic unity" while the latter remains an "anarchic assemblage

[that] shatters the filmic whole into resonant fragments" (2022, 53). While these are certainly two ways that online users could experience the film in 2021 (the time of Smith's writing), neither can match the impact of a platform that has shaped how fans have encountered, remixed, and transformed hundreds of film texts throughout the heyday of Web 2.0: Tumblr.

Founded in 2007, Tumblr quickly became known as a visual-forward micro-blogging site whose interface allowed for the seamless posting of text, links, audio, images, and video. Its central feature is not the publication of original content, but the reblogging of other users' posts. Popular posts are reblogged thousands of times, often with merely a tag or half a sentence or no new content added by the rebloggers. This endless reblogging made Tumblr what Evangelos Tziallas calls "a shared archive with no beginning and no end ... punctured with just enough repetition to make it feel familiar and stable" (2016). A lot has changed in the platform's decade and a half of existence, including being bought by Yahoo in 2013 and then by Automattic in 2019. Because of its new owners' increasing anti-sex policies, Tumblr as it was known to its early users began to fall apart in 2018, yet in its heyday, the platform was central to much queer content because of all the ways it allowed users to interact and create digital forms of self-expression (Haimson et al. 2021).

Given Tumblr's rapid demise as the site for overly emotional posts and bite-sized pornography, the specific examples I can quote here are limited and much more recent than those I remember from a decade ago. Readers active on the platform will surely remember even more posts like the ones I discuss here. I have selected these examples because they illustrate the types of affective responses users had to these excerpts from the film. Fan-created posts about *Y Tu Mamá También* varied widely in form, type, and tone: from GIF collections to montage vids to fanart. The creators of most of these posts, especially GIF collections, are difficult to ascertain because of how quickly and seamlessly these media fragments are shared, remixed, and re-shared (or re-blogged in the platform's parlance). Their reappearance over time feeds into what scholar Alex Cho has termed the "queer reverb" of Tumblr: "user-created emotional/temporal prisms that span its multiplicity and simultaneously help define it as a set of urges, wants, and hurts ... bringing Tumblrs together by means of a shared affinity" (2015, 52).

A montage vid by Tumblr user sereneblood brings together the boys' final meeting in the film, along with other scenes from the rest of the film, with the moody pop song "Old Friend" by Mitski. Every time the song's chorus hits the line "If you'll meet me at Blue Diner / I'll take coffee and talk about nothing," the video cuts to segments of Tenoch and Julio sitting at the restaurant having coffee. In between these shots, segments of the film play back as if they were a set of memories coming to the surface as the old friends share their coffee. The kiss makes an appearance during the song's second verse: "I haven't told anyone. Just like we promised / have you?" Although we know from the film narrator that such an agreement was never explicit between the two boys in the film, this remix adds a different interpretation of their fallout and final meeting, imagining an alternative version where, despite their separation, they can acknowledge how much deeper their connection originally was. Overall, the montage vid reorganizes the temporality of Tenoch and Julio's story and retells it as a story of long-lost love.

In a similar fashion, the original fanart by Tumblr user art--harridan depicts the kiss as an unspoken, unshakeable memory between the two friends. The digital art recreates the final meeting as a still image with Tenoch and Julio sitting on both sides at the bottom of the frame, not facing each other. Behind them, where the window of the restaurant would be, a close-up of their kiss occupies most of the image. The kiss is coloured in what the artist calls "an unnatural neon green glow" and the friends' faces are shaded to match this glow, as if their supersized memory were stained glass colouring the incoming sunlight.

By reimagining the story of *Y Tu Mamá También* as one of lost love, Tumblr posts like this speak more to the hopes and expectations of fans. Fanart

Figure 36
Fanart of the kiss between Tenoch and Julio by Tumblr user @art--harridan that renders the intimate moment as a scene of longing.

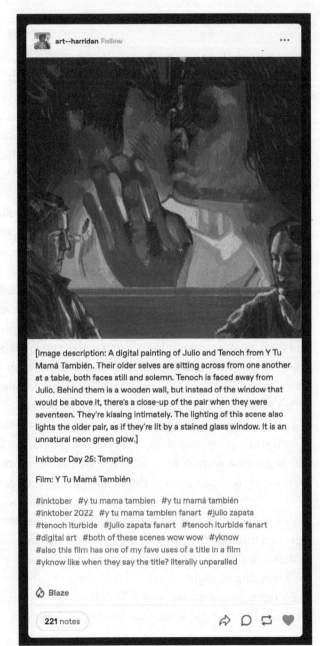

art--harridan Follow

[Image description: A digital painting of Julio and Tenoch from Y Tu Mamá También. Their older selves are sitting across from one another at a table, both faces still and solemn. Tenoch is faced away from Julio. Behind them is a wooden wall, but instead of the window that would be above it, there's a close-up of the pair when they were seventeen. They're kissing intimately. The lighting of this scene also lights the older pair, as if they're lit by a stained glass window. It is an unnatural neon green glow.]

Inktober Day 25: Tempting

Film: Y Tu Mamá También

#inktober #y tu mama tambien #y tu mamá también
#Inktober 2022 #y tu mama tamblen fanart #julio zapata
#tenoch iturbide #julio zapata fanart #tenoch iturbide fanart
#digital art #both of these scenes wow wow #yknow
#also this film has one of my fave uses of a title in a film
#yknow like when they say the title? literally unparalled

Blaze

221 notes

expresses a "context- and content-specific understanding of space and time," which simultaneously embraces "scenario over narrative and surface experience over deep identification" (Brown 2013). These paratexts extend the queer affects of the film beyond what was included in the original text, creating openings for new forms of attachment and experience. By being endlessly shared and re-shared in these networked platforms, fanart gives life to media-inspired fantasies and shapes the desire such fantasies engender as simultaneously individual and shared, internal and external, artificial and real.

Less additive yet equally transformative are the GIF sets that focus only on the kiss itself. Consider a post by Tumblr user marie-beau from January 2022, which presents the kiss broken up into five two-second GIFs. The accompanying tags to the post devolve from the informational (#Tenoch y Julio #Diego Luna #Gael García Bernal #Y tu mama tambien) to the anecdotal (#Diego Luna movie marathon) to the critical (#apparently this needs a trigger warning? #tw: kissing #tw: gay kissing #tw: suggestive #tw: shirtless #did i cover it yet? #do I jave to put trigger warnings on non-explicit straight kissing too?). While the media excerpts champion the scene that the user presumably appreciated while watching their Diego Luna movie marathon, the tags offer an impassioned response to the platform's restrictive policies for sharing the scene, including the suggestion that these restrictions are homophobic.

The user-created "emotional/temporal prisms" do not stop there. A re-blog of this post by Tumblr user misviciosycaprichos adds on the following commentary:

#no because #omfg #the tenderness #the familiarity??? #the longing???
#its PALPABLE the way this kiss was a long time coming and
    absolutely freeing to partake in just through the body language
#the way it goes from hesitant to frantic
#the whole fucking film was leading to that moment of terrifying
    realization
#and just

Figure 37
Example of a Tumblr post breaking
down the twenty-five-second kiss
into five two-second GIFs. Posted by
user @marie-beau on 8 January 2022.

#the way the desire was interspersed throughout in hints that could
     be shrugged off UUNTIL IT COULDNT
#gahhhh

Mobilizing the tags feature to structure a sort of free verse response, the user conveys their visceral reaction to viewing the scene after "the whole fucking film was leading to that moment." The user likewise foregrounds the "PAL-PABLE" affective charge of the kiss and its bodily impact on the viewer themselves ("gahhhh"). I would argue the post is reacting not only to the scene itself, or to the user's memory of first watching the scene, but to the *form* in which the scene is parcelled and presented here. The five two-second-long GIFs break up the original scene's tension into furtive gestures while, at the same time, inviting the viewer to dwell on each gesture given the GIFs' continuous repetition. If, for this user, the sensual power of the scene was its buildup and seeming inevitability, the broken-up yet repetitive segments of the scene only exacerbate the buildup's intensity and temporality.

It is no mistake that GIFs have been characterized as "promiscuous" (Eppink 2014). GIFs are "distillations of pure affect," capturing a set of feelings through infinite repetition. GIFs from film scenes are "moments plucked out of the fabric of the film, revealing the unique quality of a performance, a body, a face. The epitome of a style, the essence of a character, the allure of the film, its erotic charge, are all there for your contemplation, over and over" (Newman 2016). GIFs are also easily shared across new media platforms. As Melanie E.S. Kohnen argues, GIFs are "the visual currency of Tumblr" in how they capture audiences' favourite moments from a film and transform them into a new shared language across users (2018, 354). By creating GIF sets such as those of the Tenoch-Julio kiss, users not only comment on the original scene but also convey and circulate the sensations they originally felt when watching that moment, creating an enduring affective attachment to the original scene in the process. As "looped affect reels," these sets capture something of the scene's "visceral and affective experience" as well as the "transferred energy between onscreen and off-screen bodies" (Tziallas 2016).

The visceral and affective experience of watching these endless loops grants a new life to a film fragment that was once absent, at least for home video audiences in the United States and Canada. Despite its initial censorship, it has come back with a vengeance: cut apart, parcelled, remixed, and made infinite. Through these new media montages, the Tenoch-Julio kiss endures in popularity as it also takes on new meanings. Ushered by social media and other internet affordances, the media afterlives for that kiss help audiences reencounter the moment and their memories of watching it. At the same time, these new posts also decontextualize the cinematic moment and inscribe it with a new set of meanings. The unspoken moments in the film are suddenly suffused with newfound intimacy, desire, and longing. Across these digital media remixes, new versions of the kiss also espouse new forms of masculinity that are no longer only about virility or sexual power but also about tenderness and care.

I end this book with a sustained discussion of the Tenoch-Julio kiss because its initial reception and enduring impact chart the different analytical paths I have pursued across the previous chapters. Chapter 1 traced how the appraisal of the film's sexual daringness shifted from a morbid fascination in its initial reception to a more reserved, metaphorical evaluation to a newfound excitable appreciation twenty-plus years later. The popular responses elicited by the kiss have likewise vacillated across a positive-negative spectrum over the years. While its re-appraisal by audiences demonstrates broader changes in social mores across the twenty-first century, the kiss's staying power reveals its momentousness to be well-earned. Chapter 2 argued that the musical legacy of the film, initially thought to be tied to its alternative rock youth-oriented soundtrack, proved to lie in its pointed use of powerful melodramatic tunes. Internet users' remixing of the kiss with newer songs – evident not only in the Tumblr vids described above but also, more recently, in the burst of TikTok fan edits of the film – reveals a continued tendency towards the more melancholic longings of "Si No Te Hubieras Ido" than the abrasive beats of "Here Comes the Mayo." Chapter 3 analyzed the film's portrayal of its two men protagonists as a crucial entry point to investigate the class and ethnic politics of Mexican masculinity at the turn of the century. Fanart and other user-generated posts about the kiss likewise continue the rearticulations of masculinity engendered by the film and its protagonists' rise to stardom. In short, the media afterlives of *Y Tu Mamá También* prolong, recast, and ensconce the film's key features into opportunities for newfound desires and attachments, serving these features up for a networked audience far more geographically and demographically diverse. The interlaced coexistence of these different strands represents the multivariate queer legacy of this emblematic twenty-first-century global cinematic classic.

References

Acevedo-Muñoz, Ernesto R. 2004. "Sex, Class, and Mexico in Alfonso Cuarón's Y Tu Mamá También." *Film and History: An Interdisciplinary Journal of Film and Television Studies* 34, no. 1: 39–48.

Aguilar, Carlos. 2021. "When 'Y Tu Mamá También' Changed Everything." *New York Times*, 25 August. https://www.nytimes.com/2021/08/25/movies/y-tu-mama-tambien.html.

Aguilera Skvirsky, Salomé. 2020. "Must the Subaltern Speak? On *Roma* and the Cinema of Domestic Service." *FORMA* 1, no. 2: 1–34.

Alvarado, Eduardo. 2001. "Es muy divertida y aleccionadora." *Reforma*, 8 June, 21.

Arredondo, Arturo. 2001. "'Y Tu Mamá También,' de Alfonso Cuaron." *Novedades*, 26 June, 12.

Aviña, Rafael. 2001. "Cuarón al desnudo." *Reforma*, 8 June, 4.

Ayala Blanco, Jorge. 2001. "Cuarón y la franqueza juvenil." *El Financiero*, 11 June, 102.

Baer, Hester, and Ryan Long. 2004. "Transnational Cinema and the Mexican State in Alfonso Cuarón's *Y Tu Mamá También*." *South Central Review* 21, no. 3: 150–68.

Barbas-Rhoden, Laura. 2019. "The Representation of Slow Violence and the Spatiality of Injustice in *Y tu mamá también* and *Temporada de patos*." In *Ecofictions, Ecorealities, and Slow Violence in Latin America and the Latinx*

World, edited by Ana María Mutis, Elizabeth Pettinaroli, and Ilka Kressner, 95–113. New York: Routledge.

Baugh, Scott. 2019. *Y Tu Mamá También: Mythologies of Youth*. New York: Routledge.

Benedict, Raquel S. 2021. "Everyone Is Beautiful and No One Is Horny." *Blood Knife*, February 14. https://bloodknife.com/everyone-beautiful-no-one-horny/.

Benson-Allott, Caetlin. 2009. "Sex versus the Small Screen: Home Video Censorship and Alfonso Cuarón's *Y Tu Mamá También*." *Jump Cut* 51. http://www.ejumpcut.org/archive/jc51.2009/tuMamaTambien/.

Bersani, Leo. 1987. "Is the Rectum a Grave?" *October* 43: 197–222.

Bertrán, Dorian Lugo. 2009. "Alfonso Cuarón y la producción fílmica latino-queer." *DeSignis* 14: 50–61.

Brown, Lyndsay. 2013. "Pornographic Space-time and the Potential of Fantasy in Comics and Fan Art." *Transformative Works and Cultures* 13: 1–28.

Calderón, Santiago. 2001. "El rock pone voz al cine." *Reforma*, 20 July, 24.

Calva Gomez, Araceli. "Los de Molotov no saben decir 'no.'" *Milenio*, 26 May 2001, 5.

Carroll, Amy Sara. 2012. "Global Mexico's Coproduction: Babel, Pan's Labyrinth, and Children of Men." *Journal of Transnational American Studies* 4, no. 2: 1–30.

Castillo, Alberto. 2001. "No se meten con su mama." *Reforma*, 28 June, 14.

Celin, Fernando. 2001. "Tres en el paraíso, una en el misterio." *Novedades*, 24 June 2001, 8.

Chapman, Wilson, June Dry, and Ryan Lattanzio. "The 22 Sexiest Queer Movies of All Time." *IndieWire*, 7 June 2023. https://www.indiewire.com/gallery/sexy-lgbtq-queer-movies-lesbian-gay-romance/y-tu-mama-tambien-diego-luna-gael-garcia-bernal-2001-2/.

Cho, Alexander. 2015. "Queer Reverb: Tumblr, Affect, Time." In *Networked Affect*, edited by Ken Hills, Susanna Paasonen, and Michael Petit, 43–58. Cambridge: MIT Press.

Chung, Hye Jean. 2011. "Cinema as Archeology: The Acousmêtre and the Multiple Layering of Temporality and Spatiality." *Contemporaneity: Historical Presence in Visual Culture* 1: 105–16.

Cole, Shaun. 2012. *The Story of Men's Underwear*. New York: Parkstone International.

Contreras, Rosa. 2001. "Alfonso Cuarón regresa al cine con *Y Tu Mamá También*." *Novedades*, 26 May, 7.

Corliss, Richard. 2007. "Learning Pedro Infante." *TIME*, 15 April. https://content.time.com/time/arts/article/0,8599,1610682,00.html.

Cuarón, Alfonso, and Carlos Cuarón. 2001. *Y Tu Mamá También: Guión y Argumento Cinematográfico*. Mexico City: Trilce Ediciones.

Davalos, Patricia E. 2001. "*Y tu mamá también* retrata al México más joven y urgido." *La Crónica*, 26 May, 31.

Davis, Nick. 2014. "I Love You, *Hombre*: *Y Tu Mamá También* as Border-Crossing Bromance" In *Reading the Bromance: Homosocial Relationships in Film and Television*, edited by Micheal DeAngelis, 109–38. Detroit: Wayne State University Press.

De la Garza, Armida. 2009. "Realism and National Identity in *Y Tu Mamá También*: An Audience Perspective." In *Realism and the Audiovisual Media*, edited by Lucia Nagib and Cecilia Mello, 108–18. New York: Palgrave Macmillan.

De la Mora, Sergio. 2009. *Cinemachismo: Masculinities and Sexuality in Mexican Film*. Austin: University of Texas Press.

De la Torriente, Eugenia. 2001. "Un Pedro Infante para el Siglo XXI." *El Nacional*, 2 December, 1.

Dickinson, Kay. 2008. *Off Key: When Film and Music Won't Work Together*. Oxford: Oxford University Press.

Domínguez-Ruvalcaba, Héctor. 2007. *Modernity and the Nation in Mexican Representations of Masculinity: From Sensuality to Bloodshed*. New York: Palgrave Macmillan.

Donapetry, Maria. 2004. "And Your Motherland Too: The Body of the

Spanish Woman in *Y Tu Mamá Tambien* (And Your Mother Too)." *South Central Review* 21, no. 3: 150–68.

Dorantes, Jorge. 2001a. "Por que es grande *Y Tu Mamá También*." *El Economista*, 25 May, 59.

– 2001b. "*Y tu mamá también*: olvidemos el escándalo." *El Economista*, 8 June, 51.

Dunkley, Cathy. 2000. "Good Machine Revs Expansion." *Hollywood Reporter*, 18 May, 1–2.

El Universal. 2002. "*Y Tu Mamá También* abre ciclo chileno de cine erótico." *El Universal*, 12 April, E13.

Eppink, Jason. 2014. "A Brief History of the GIF (So Far)." *Journal of Visual Culture* 13, no. 3: 298–306.

Ezra, Elizabeth, and Terry Rowden. 2006. "What Is Transnational Cinema?" In *Transnational Cinema: The Film Reader*, edited by Elizabeth Ezra and Terry Rowden, 1–12. New York: Routledge.

Fabian, Monika. 2013. "Molotov's Hollow Gesture of Solidarity after 'Puto' Controversy." *ABC News*, 8 August. https://abcnews.go.com/ABC_Univision/Opinion/molotovs-hollow-gesture-solidarity-puto-contro versy/story?id=19904640.

Feinstein, Howard. 2002. "Mexican Rave." *Guardian*, 10 April. https://www.theguardian.com/culture/2002/apr/10/artsfeatures.

Finnegan, Nuala. 2007. "'So What's Mexico Really Like?': Framing the Local, Negotiating the Global in Alfonso Cuarón's *Y Tu Mamá También*." In *Contemporary Latin American Cinema: Breaking into the Global Market*, edited by Deborah Shaw, 29–50. Lanham: Rowman and Littlefield.

Franco, Rene. 2001. "Y el soundtrack ... también." *El Economista*, 12 June, 55.

Freeman, Elizabeth. 2010. *Time Binds: Queer Temporalities, Queer Histories*. Durham: Duke University Press.

Frost, David, host. 2013. *The Frost Interview*. Season 2, Episode 8, "Gael García Bernal." Aired 4 October, on Al Jazeera English. https://www.al

jazeera.com/program/the-frost-interview/2013/10/5/gael-garcia-bernal-being-optimistic.

García, Juan Carlos. 2001. "Hacen un álbum de película." *Reforma*, 26 May, 14.

– 2003. "Se ve y se oye. La Industria de las bandas sonoras." *Reforma*, 12 September, 18.

García Tsao, Leonardo. 2001a. "Solo con tu pajero." *La Jornada*, 22 June, 15.

– 2001b. "Film Reviews: 'And Your Mother Too.'" *Variety*, 24 June. https://variety.com/2001/film/awards/and-your-mother-too-1200468654/.

Gomes, Carlee. 2023. "The Puritanical Eye: Hyper-Mediation, Sex on Film, and the Disavowal of Desire." *Lo Specchio Scuro*, 25 November. https://specchioscuro.it/the-puritanical-eye-hyper-mediation-sex-on-film-and-the-disavowal-of-desire/.

Gray, Timothy M. 2003. "Eye on the Oscars: Academy Speaking in Tongues." *Variety*, 13 January, A2.

Haimson, Oliver L., Avery Dame-Griff, Elias Capello, and Zahari Richter. 2021. "Tumblr Was a Trans Technology: The Meaning, Importance, History, and Future of Trans Technologies." *Feminist Media Studies* 21, no. 3: 345–61.

Hammer, Mauricio. 2001a. "Encuentros y desencuentros." *Reforma*, 8 June, 45.

– 2001b. "Matrimonio por conveniencia." *Reforma*, 20 July, 24.

Harris, Dana, and Carl DiOrio. 2002. "Good Machine Buy Alters Focus at U." *Variety*, 2 May. https://variety.com/2002/film/markets-festivals/good-machine-buy-alters-focus-at-u-1117866379/.

Hernandez, Raoul. 2002. "Y Tu Mamá También: Record Review." *Austin Chronicle*, 17 May. https://www.austinchronicle.com/music/2002-05-17/86601/.

Higbee, Will, and Song Hwee Lim. 2010. "Concepts of Transnational Cinema: Towards a Critical Transnationalism in Film Studies." *Transnational Cinemas* 1, no. 1: 7–22.

Higson, Andrew. 2006. "The Limiting Imagination of National Cinema." In *Transnational Cinema: The Film Reader*, edited by Elizabeth Ezra and Terry Rowden, 15–26. New York: Routledge.

Hilderbrand, Lucas. 2009. *Inherent Vice: Bootleg Histories of Videotape and Copyright*. Durham: Duke University Press.

Hind, Emily. 2004a. "Post-NAFTA Mexican Cinema, 1998–2002." *Studies in Latin American Popular Culture* 23: 95–111.

– 2004b. "Provincia in Recent Mexican Cinema, 1989–2004." *Discourse* 26, no. 1–2: 26–45.

Hirschberg, Lynn. 2003. "The Way We Live Now: Questions for Alfonso Cuarón." *New York Times Magazine*, 23 March, 15.

Hoy. 2002. "*Y Tu Mamá También* se estrena en Inglaterra." 11 April, 2B.

Huerta, César. 2001. "Solo para adultos." *Reforma*, 11 June, 11.

– 2009. "El no quiere ser Pedro Infante (ni Jorge Negrete)." *El Universal*, 18 May, 1.

Irwin, Robert McKee. 2003. *Mexican Masculinities*. Minneapolis: University of Minnesota Press.

Jiménez, Pilar. 2002. "Atrae 'Mama' a asiáticos." *Reforma*, 13 April, 5.

Kennedy, John R. 2012. "TIFF Hit 'Pause' 11 Years Ago." *Global News*, 11 September. https://globalnews.ca/news/285320/tiff-hit-pause-11-years-ago/.

Kohnen, Melanie E.S. 2018. "Tumblr Pedagogies." In *A Companion to Media Fandom and Fan Studies*, edited by Paul Booth, 351–67. London: Wiley & Sons.

Kowalski, Jan, and Jerzy Nowak. 2016. "Circumcision: Systematic Review and Meta-analysis." *ARC Journal of Urology* 1, no. 2: 1–8.

Kwon, Jungmin. 2022. "The Commercialization and Popularization of Boys Love in South Korea." In *Queer Transfigurations: Boys Love Media in Asia*, edited by James Welker, 80–91. Honolulu: University of Hawaii Press.

Lahr-Vivaz, Elena. 2006. "Unconsummated Fictions and Virile Voiceovers." *Revista de Estudios Hispánicos* 40, no. 1: 79–101.

Leal, Franklin. 2004. "Gael 'Calienta' Sundance." *Milenio*, 19 January, 8.

León, Magaly. 2001. "Una mirada honesta a la adolescencia." *uno más uno*, 16 June, 16.

Lee, Chris. "2018 Is the Year of Prestige Peen." *Vulture*, 29 November 2018. https://www.vulture.com/2018/11/2018-is-the-year-of-prestige-peen.html.

Lilley, Sandra, Gwen Aviles, and Monica Castillo. 2019. "'Roma' Earned Alfonso Cuarón His Second Best Director Award. Here's Why." NBC *News*, 24 February. https://www.nbcnews.com/storyline/oscars/roma-earned-alfonso-cuar-n-his-second-best-director-award-n974551.

Llamas-Rodriguez, Juan. 2023. "The Return of Indigenismo in Netflix Mexico." In *Streaming Video: Storytelling across Borders*, edited by Amanda Lotz and Ramon Lobato, 225–47. New York: New York University Press.

López, Tomás. 2006. "Gael: Ser o no ser mexicano." *El Sol de México*, 4 October, 1.

Maher, Kevin, and Alex Hess. "The 37 Best Sex Movies Ever Made: A Countdown." *Esquire*, 2 March 2023. https://www.esquire.com/uk/culture/film/a7509/best-sex-movies/.

Martínez Assad, Carlos. 1992. "Breve diccionario de 'ayalismos' sobre mujeres y cine." *Debate Feminista* 5: 321–4.

Melche, Julia Elena. 2001. "Jocosa, ironica e inteligente." *Reforma*, 10 June, 5.

Mendoza de Lira, Alejandra. 2000. "No me siento el DiCaprio mexicano." *El Universal*, 10 February, 7.

Menne, Jeff. 2007. "A Mexican Nouvelle Vague: The Logic of New Waves under Globalization." *Cinema Journal* 47, no. 1: 70–92.

Milenio. 2001. "Las actuaciones la salvan." 10 June, 12.

Miller, Toby, Freya Schiwy, and Marta Hernández-Salván. 2012. "Distribution, the Forgotten Element in Transnational Cinema." *Transnational Cinemas* 3, no. 1: 197–214.

Monsiváis, Carlos. 1995. "Mythologies." Translated by Ana M. Lopez. In *Mexican Cinema*, edited by Paulo Antonio Paranagua, 117–27. London: British Film Institute.

—2001. "Lo local y lo global." *El Norte*, 21 October, 1.

—2006. "El cine mexicano." *Bulletin of Latin American Research* 25, no. 4: 512–16.

—2013. "Soñadora, coqueta y ardiente. Notas sobre sexismo en la literatura mexicana." In *Misogino Feminista*, 21–44. Mexico: Debate Feminista/ Oceano.

Naime, X Andrés. 2001. "Y Tu Mamá También." *uno más uno*, 1 June, 21.

Noble, Andrea. 2005. *Mexican National Cinema*. London: Routledge.

Oropesa, Salvador A. 2008. "Proxemics, Homogenization, and Diversity in Mexico's Road Movies: *Por la Libre* (2000), *Sin dejar Huella* (2000), and *Y Tu Mamá También* (2001)." *Hispanic Issues On Line* 3, no. 5: 92–112.

Puerta, Ramiro. 2001. "Y Tu Mamá También." *Toronto International Film Festival Guide*, 185.

Quintanilla, Felipe Q. 2014. "La Llorona como esfinge subversiva en 'Y Tu Mamá También' (2002) de Alfonso Cuaron." *Chasqui* 43, no. 1: 132–46.

Rangel, Ivett, Omar Cabrera, and Cesar Huerta. 2001. "Triunfan los 'Charo-lastras.'" *Reforma*, 10 September, G1.

Reid, Joe. 2017. "15 Years Later, 'Y Tu Mamá También' Still Has the Hottest 3-Way Sex Scene in Movie History." *Decider*, 17 March, https://decider.com/2017/03/17/y-tu-mama-tambien-hottest-three-way-sex-scene-ever/.

Reinstein, Mara. 2022. "The Short-Lived Reign of MTV's Best Kiss Award." *Ringer*, 2 June. https://www.theringer.com/movies/2022/6/2/23150508/mtv-movie-awards-best-kiss-history.

Reyes, Salvador Franco. 2004. "Se Rebela." *El Universal*, 19 May, E1.

Rock, Chava. 2003. "La banda sonora de *Y Tu Mamá También* Candidata al Grammy." *La Jornada*, 3 February, 6.

Rousselot, Fabrice. 2004. "T'es qui, là?" *Liberation*, 15 May, 52.

Rubenstein, Anne. 2001. "Bodies, Cities, Cinema: Pedro Infante's Death as Political Spectacle." In *Fragments of a Golden Age: The Politics of Culture in Mexico since 1940*, edited by Gilbert Joseph, Anne Rubenstein, Eric Zolov, 199–233. Durham: Duke University Press.

Saldaña-Portillo, María Josefina. 2005. "In the Shadow of NAFTA: 'Y Tu Mamá También' Revisits the National Allegory of Mexican Sovereignty." *American Quarterly 57*, no. 3: 751–77.

San Filippo, Maria. 2013. *The B Word: Bisexuality in Contemporary Film and Television*. Bloomington: Indiana University Press.

Sánchez Barajas, Karla Paulina. 2016. *El Rock en el Cine Mexicano: de Leitmotiv a Soundtrack*. Mexicali: Universidad Autónoma de Baja California.

Sánchez Prado, Ignacio. 2013. "The Neoliberal Stars: Salma Hayek, Gael García Bernal and the Post-Mexican Film Icon." In *Latin American Icons: Fame across Borders*, edited by Dianna C. Niebylski and Patrick O'Connor, 147–56. Nashville: Vanderbilt University Press.

– 2014. *Screening Neoliberalism: Transforming Mexican Cinema, 1988–2012*. Nashville: Vanderbilt University Press.

– 2018. "Special Dossier on Alfonso Cuarón's Roma: Class Trouble." *Mediático*, 24 December. http://reframe.sussex.ac.uk/mediatico/2018/12/24/special-dossier-on-alfonso-cuarons-roma-class-trouble/.

Segoviano, Rogelio. 2004. "El animal cinemático: Gael Garcia." *Diario Monitor*, 30 September, 1B.

Smith, Paul Julian. 2002. "Heaven's Mouth." *Sight and Sound* 12, no. 4: 16–19.

– 2003. "Transatlantic Traffic in Recent Mexican Films." *Journal of Latin American Cultural Studies* 12, no. 3: 389–400.

– 2017. *Queer Mexico: Cinema and Television since the 2000s*. Detroit: Wayne State University Press.

– 2022. *Y Tu Mamá También*. London: Bloomsbury.

Smith, Krista. 2005. "Vanity Fair's 2005 Hollywood Portfolio." *Vanity Fair*, March, 361–401.

Solórzano, Fernanda. 2002. "La última carcajada de Cuarón." *Letras Libres* 4, no. 41: 92–3.

Tierney, Dolores, Victoria Ruetalo, and Roberto Carlos Ortiz. 2017. "New Latin-American Stardom, the Local/Global Stars of Latin American Cinema's New 'Golden Age': Sonia Braga, Gael Garcia Bernal, and Ricardo

Darin." In *Routledge Guide to Latin American Cinemas*, edited by Marvin D'Lugo, Ana Lopez, and Laura Podalsky, 164–79. New York: Routledge.

Tierney, Dolores. 2018. *New Transnationalisms in Contemporary Latin American Cinemas*. Edinburgh: Edinburgh University Press.

Torres San Martín, Patricia. 2011. *Cine, Género y Jóvenes*. Guadalajara: Universidad de Guadalajara.

– 2016. "Y Tu Mamá También." In *Clásicos del Cine Mexicano*, edited by Christian Wehr, 501–18. Madrid: Iberoamericana.

Tziallas, Evangelos. 2016. "Pornophilia: Porn Gifs, Fandom, Circuitries." *Porn Studies* 3, no. 3: 311–13.

Worrell, M.S. 2011. "Sexual Awakenings and the Malignant Fictions of Masculinity in Alfonso Cuarón's *Y Tu Mamá También*." In *Sex and the Citizen: Interrogating the Caribbean*, edited by Faith Smith, 157–67. Charlottesville: University of Virginia Press.

Yoshida, Emily. 2018. "At Venice, Roma's Male Nudity Doesn't Play for Laughs." *Vulture*, 31 August. https://www.vulture.com/2018/08/venice-roma-male-nudity-doesnt-play-for-laughs.html.

Mediography

American Pie 2. J.B. Rogers. USA. 2001. 108 min.

Amores Perros. Alejandro González Iñárritu. Mexico. 2000. 154 min.

"Beautiful Soul." 2004. Written by Adam Watts and Andy Dodd. Performed by Jesse McCartney. Hollywood Records.

Beavis and Butt-Head. MTV. USA. 1993–2011. 15 min.

"By This River." 1977. Written by Brian Eno, Dieter Moebius, and Hans-Joachim Roedelius. Performed by Brian Eno. BMG Records.

Club de Cuervos. Netflix. Mexico. 2015–19. 40 min.

"Cold Air." 2001. Written by Natalie Imbruglia, Liam Coverdale-Howe, Chris Corner, and Ian Pickering. Performed by Natalie Imbruglia. RCA Records.

Desenfrenadas. Netflix. Mexico. 2020. 43 min.

Doña Herlinda y su Hijo. Jaime Humberto Hermosillo. Mexico. 1985. 90 min.

El Crimen del Padre Amaro. Carlos Carrera. Mexico. 2002. 118 min.

El Laberinto del Fauno. Guillermo del Toro. Mexico. 2006. 118 min.

El Lugar sin Límites. Arturo Ripstein. 1978. 110 min.

"Glorious." 2007. Written by Natalie Imbruglia and Crispin Hunt. Performed by Natalie Imbruglia. Brightside Records.

"Here Comes the Mayo." 2001. Written by Paco Ayala, Randy Ebright, Tito Fuentes, Miky Huidobro, Barry Ashworth, and Jason O'Bryan. Performed by Molotov and Dub Pistols. Universal Music.

Jules et Jim. François Truffaut. France. 1962. 105 min.

La Mala Educación. Pedro Almodóvar. Spain. 2004. 106 min.

"La Sirenita." 2001. Written by Rigo Tovar. Performed by Plastilina Mosh and Tonino Carotone. EMI Music.

"La Tumba Será el Final." 2001. Written by Felipe Vidal. Performed by Flaco Jiménez and Freddy Ojeda. EMI Music.

Les Valseuses. Bertrand Blier. France. 1974. 118 min.

Luis Miguel: La Serie. Netflix. Mexico. 2018–21. 60 min.

Milk. Gus Van Sant. USA. 2008. 128 min.

"Old Friend." 2018. Written by Mitski Mayawaki. Performed by Mitski. Dead Oceans.

"Puto." 1997. Written by Tito Fuentes. Performed by Molotov. Universal Music.

¿Qué Te Ha Dado Esa Mujer? Ismael Rodríguez. Mexico. 1951. 100 min.

¿Quién Mató a Sara? Netflix. Mexico. 2021–2. 40 min.

Roma. Alfonso Cuarón. Mexico. 2018. 135 min.

Sense8. Netflix. USA. 2015–18. 60 min.

"Si No Te Hubieras Ido." 1999. Written by Marco Antonio Solís. Performed by Marco Antonio Solís. Fonovisa.

Sólo con Tu Pareja. Alfonso Cuarón. Mexico. 1991. 94 min.

"Watermelon in Easter Hay." 1979. Written by Frank Zappa. Performed by Frank Zappa. Zappa Records.

Index